32

Conserving and Protecting Water

What You Can Do

GREEN ISSUES IN FOCUS

Stephen Feinstein

Enslow Publishers, Inc.
40 Industrial Road
Box 398
Berkeley Heights, NJ 07922
USA

http://www.enslow.com

Library of Congress Cataloging-in-Publication Data

Feinstein, Stephen.
    Conserving and protecting water : what you can do / Stephen Feinstein.
        p. cm. — (Green issues in focus)
    Includes bibliographical references and index.
    Summary: "Read about global water scarcity and pollution, federal regulations and
standards for water quality in the United States, and what you can do to help"—Provided
by publisher.
    ISBN 978-0-7660-3346-7
    1. Water conservation—Juvenile literature. 2. Water-supply—Juvenile literature. 3. Water
pollution—Juvenile literature. 4. Environmental protection—Juvenile literature.
    I. Title.
    TD388.F45 2010
    363.6'1—dc22

                        2009054327

Printed in the United States of America

052010 Lake Book Manufacturing, Inc., Melrose Park, IL

10 9 8 7 6 5 4 3 2 1

To Our Readers: We have done our best to make sure all Internet addresses in this book were active
and appropriate when we went to press. However, the author and the publisher have no control over
and assume no liability for the material available on those Internet sites or on other Web sites they
may link to. Any comments or suggestions can be sent by e-mail to comments@enslow.com or to the
address on the back cover.

♻ Enslow Publishers, Inc., is committed to printing our books on recycled paper. The paper in
every book contains 10% to 30% post-consumer waste (PCW). The cover board on the outside of
each book contains 100% PCW. Our goal is to do our part to help young people and the environment too!

Illlustration Credits: Associated Press, pp. 5, 8, 33, 45, 51, 54, 67, 72, 85, 90, 96, 105, 116; John M.
Evans, U.S. Geological Survey/U.S. Department of the Interior, p. 14; Peggy Greb, U.S. Department
of Agriculture/Agricultural Research Service, p. 16; National Aeronautics and Space Administration,
p. 29; National Oceanic and Atmospheric Administration, pp. 62, 117; National Resources
Conservation Service, p. 57; Shutterstock, pp. 3, 11, 21, 24, 39, 78, 82, 101, 112, 115, 118, 119; Vestergaard
Frandsen, pp. 74, 117; © Wave Royalty Free/Alamy, p. 108; Wikimedia Commons, p. 14.

Cover Illustration: Associated Press. (Photo shows a shepherd in southern India on the dry bed of
the Himayatsagar reservoir in 2005.)

Contents

1. Global Access to Water 4

2. Problems of Water Scarcity 23

3. Water Pollution 49

4. Water Quality and Public Health 66

5. Protecting Our Water 84

6. What You Can Do to Help 104

Chapter Notes 115

Glossary 120

For More Information 123

Further Reading 124

Internet Addresses 125

Index 126

Global Access to Water

Can you imagine putting dirty water into a ceramic pot and having it come out ready to drink? That is what happens with a water-purifying device promoted by Ron Rivera for use in the Third World, where clean drinking water is desperately needed. Rivera says, "You put dirty water in—gray water that many communities still drink—and it comes out crystal clear." Rivera called his ceramic water filters "weapons of biological mass destruction"[1] because they kill germs that cause illness. Rivera spent twenty-five years visiting many poor villages throughout much of the Third World. Wherever he went in Africa, Asia, and Latin America, he worked with potters, showing them how to make the filters.

Tracy Hawkins makes clay water filters in her ceramics studio for use in developing countries.

Rivera's device resembles a big terra-cotta flowerpot. This ceramic water filter was invented by a Guatemalan chemist named Fernando Mazariegos. The pot is made of clay mixed with sawdust or ground rice husks. When the pot is fired, the sawdust or rice husks burn away, leaving small pores. Water is able to seep through the pores. But the bacteria in the water cannot pass through the tiny pores. After firing, the filter is coated with a silver solution. The coating kills more than 98 percent of contaminants that cause diarrhea, a leading cause of death in the Third World. Thanks to Rivera's filters, the incidence of diarrhea is cut in half. This is a great benefit to children, who are especially vulnerable to this disease. The ceramic filter fits into a five-gallon container that collects the water. The container is fitted with a spigot. The ceramic filter can purify one to three quarts of water an hour.

Rivera set up small businesses to produce the water filters in many countries. These included Ghana, Cambodia, Yemen, and Colombia. His factories have produced about three hundred thousand filters, used by about 1.5 million people.

Water: An Essential Resource

In the United States, we tend to take clean water for granted. It is always available from faucets when we are thirsty or when we want to take a shower. But this is not the case in many other parts of the world. In much of Africa, people have to walk several miles for their water. In the more arid areas it is necessary to walk even farther. Sometimes all they find is a pond with slimy water. Waterborne diseases such as typhoid and cholera are common. An enormous number of people in Africa, more than 90 percent of that continent's population, have to dig in the ground for their water. Where the wells are very deep, people have to line up in human chains to bring up the water.[2]

> **In much of Africa, people have to walk several miles for their water.**

Africa is not the only place where lack of access to freshwater threatens the health and livelihoods of millions of people. The water crisis is everywhere, on every continent and in cities large and small. Water is in crisis in China, in Southeast Asia, in the American Southwest. Parts of Europe also face shortages. Droughts have become more widespread and water tables have been dropping. When wetlands become dry, the groundwater becomes polluted with contaminants. In other areas, rain comes so hard and fast in sudden downpours that flooding occurs. In the blink of an eye, rivers become raging torrents.

Water is absolutely essential for the earth's unique characteristic—the presence of life. Of course, the planet's amazing diversity of living organisms includes us. Freshwater is essential to human health, agriculture, industry, and natural ecosystems.

A mother and child in Zimbabwe carry water from a well to their home.

But we do not have an infinite supply of freshwater. Already, over one billion people (one in every six) around the world do not have access to clean drinking water.[3] It is estimated that by the year 2025, 5.7 billion people will suffer from water shortages. That adds up to two-thirds of the world's population. So it is easy to see that access to freshwater is becoming one of the most serious problems we face.

Water Is Us

Those of us who have had easy access to fresh water all our lives have gotten very used to its availability. But have you ever wondered why water is so incredibly important to us? Did you know that each one of us is mostly made up of water? Consider these facts: The human body is about 60 percent water by weight. Our blood is 83 percent water. Our lungs are 90 percent water. And our brain is 70 percent water.[4] Even our food is mostly water.

Not surprisingly, we need to consume an adequate amount of water to maintain our existence. A bare minimum of 0.6 gallons of water, either from drinking or from food, is a daily requirement. On average, most people in the United States do not drink more than a gallon a day. These same people use almost a hundred gallons a day to wash and flush the toilet.

In contrast, in Africa, the average person uses just under one gallon of water a day.[5]

To satisfy the daily food and clothing needs of each person, agriculture and industry require incredibly huge amounts of water. It takes about twenty-five gallons of water to grow a pound of wheat, and forty-nine gallons for a pound of apples. It takes 1,630 gallons to produce a pound of pork and 5,214 gallons to produce a pound of beef.[6] A lot of water is also used in the automobile industry, where about 105,000 gallons of water are required to make a single car.[7] And today's high-tech industry in the United States uses about 8.75 gallons of water to produce each computer memory chip.[8]

Water World

Earth is the only planet in the solar system that has liquid water on its surface. Indeed, most of Earth's surface is covered with water—so much water that the planet appears blue from space. Yet much of our blue planet is either already in the midst of, or will soon be, facing a freshwater scarcity crisis. For many of us, freshwater is still a seemingly abundant resource on the earth. But is it really? How much water is there?

Arthur C. Clarke, the author of *2001: A Space Odyssey,* once said: "How inappropriate to call this planet Earth, when clearly it is Ocean."[9] Indeed, when viewed from space, the earth

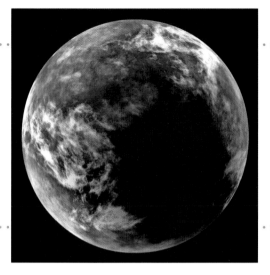

There is so much water on Earth's surface that the planet appears blue from space.

appears to be a water planet or water world. Its most prominent features are its oceans and white wisps of clouds. The vast blue bodies of water cover about 70 percent of the planet's surface. The volume of water is estimated at 333 million cubic miles.[10] Such a huge quantity might lead you to believe that there is an infinite supply of water on this planet. But how much of the earth's water is actually usable?

The oceans make up about 96.5 percent of Earth's water. Much of the remaining 3.5 percent of all water that is not salt water is frozen in glaciers and polar ice. So that does not leave very much water for use by humans. In fact, less than 0.08 of 1 percent of all of the Earth's water is accessible to us.

But according to writer Jeffrey Rothfeder,

> Even that amount is dwindling, and not only be-
> cause of thirsty people. Individual humans use

less than 10 percent of our planet's fresh water. Much more, from 60 to 70 percent, goes to irrigation, and the rest is taken up by industry.… And while dozens of studies predict what future water requirements will be, the consensus is that the total amount of water needed for people, for production of food for the swelling population, and for industry will increase by as much as 45 percent in the next twenty years.[11]

So in some places we are beginning to run out of water. Some of the earth's major rivers are running dry. The Nile in Egypt, the Ganges in India and Bangladesh, the Indus in Pakistan, the Yellow River in China, and the Colorado in the United States no longer always make it all the way to the sea. Indeed, according to former U.S. Senator Paul Simon, "the Colorado is so used up on its way to the sea that only a bubbling trickle reaches its dried-up delta at the head of the Gulf of California, and then only in wet years."[12]

Where Does Freshwater Come From?

Earth has a finite supply of freshwater, stored in underground reservoirs, surface waters, and the atmosphere. Freshwater is renewable only by rainfall or snow. This produces 9.6 to 12 cubic miles (40 to 50 cubic kilometers) per year.

Groundwater lies underground in the earth beneath our feet. All groundwater can be found within only a few miles of the surface. Groundwater makes up about 97 percent of all freshwater that is not trapped in ice. Moving groundwater circulates as part of the water cycle. The water moves underground and feeds above-ground streams, rivers, and lakes.

An area of land and all of the water associated with it, including groundwater and water on the surface, is known as a watershed. The surface water includes lakes, streams, rivers, reservoirs, and wetlands. The watershed drains all the streams and rainfall to a common outlet such as the mouth of a bay. Watersheds can be large, such as the Chesapeake Bay area. This watershed includes all the land surrounding the bay, and the rivers and streams that drain the land and empty into the bay where it enters the Atlantic Ocean. Watersheds can also be very small, and large watersheds can contain smaller ones.

Most of the groundwater is stored in aquifers—underground water reservoirs.

Many aquifers are closed systems. This means that the water within them is kept in place by layers of impermeable rock above and below the water. The water cannot penetrate the rock. In such confined, or artesian, aquifers, the water, trapped between the two layers of rock, cannot escape upward. The water in an artesian aquifer is under pressure. When a well is drilled down into the aquifer, the water rises to the surface with great force.

Other aquifers are unconfined. In such aquifers, the water rises to the level of the water table. The water table marks the

The Water Cycle

The sun causes water from the oceans and water systems on land to evaporate. The water vapor rises and condenses to form clouds. The wind disperses the clouds over the land and sea. The clouds cool and produce precipitation in the form of rain or snow; most of it falls on the oceans. Some of the water that falls on land evaporates again. Some flows back into the sea through rivers and lakes. Water is always flowing either into or out of rivers and lakes, so the amount of water in these bodies is constantly changing. The rest of the precipitation finds its way into the ground-water. This process is known as the hydrological cycle or water cycle. Humans, animals, and plants are part of the water cycle, since they need water to survive. Since life depends on water, especially freshwater, all organisms live where water is accessible.

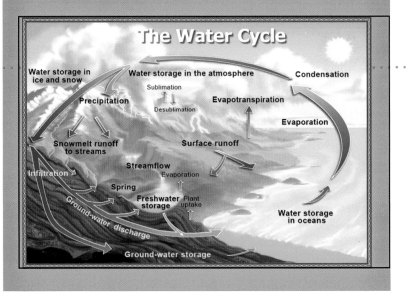

14

boundary between an area saturated with water below and an unsaturated area above. A well can be drilled down into the aquifer without having to pass through an impermeable layer of rock.

Aquifers vary in thickness from several feet to hundreds of feet. And aquifers vary in size. Some are narrow strips, while others cover hundreds of thousands of square miles under the ground. Some aquifers are only a few feet below the surface. Other aquifers are hundreds of feet below it. But most aquifers are too deep for practical use.

Groundwater in aquifers is the main source of freshwater for many countries around the world. In the United States, about half the drinking water and a quarter of the water used for all other purposes is groundwater. Unfortunately, in many parts of the world, the water is being extracted at a faster pace than it is being replenished. Without replenishment, the aquifers will run dry. Various parts of the United States face this scary outcome.

The Ogallala aquifer stretches from Texas to South Dakota, covering about 190,000 square miles (almost 500,000 square kilometers) of the Great Plains. Scientists estimate that it contains 4 trillion tons of water. This huge water source actually has 20 percent more water than Lake Huron. Indeed, the Ogallala aquifer is the largest single source of water in North America. More than two hundred thousand wells each take out about thirteen gallons of water a minute from the Ogallala aquifer.[13] This water is being used to irrigate about one-fifth of the nation's farmland. At this rate, the water in the aquifer is being depleted fourteen times faster than it is being replenished by the hydrological cycle. The Ogallala aquifer is now irrigating half as many crops as it did in the 1970s. But the demand for its water continues to grow.

Scientists estimate that more than half of the Ogallala aquifer's water is already gone. In just a few decades, the aquifer has lost a volume of water equal to the annual flow of eighteen Colorado Rivers. Cities and towns across parts of the Southwest could go dry in 10 to 20 years. Among these are major cities such as El Paso and San Antonio in Texas, and Albuquerque in New Mexico.

An agricultural engineer calculates the irrigation schedule for a cotton field in Arizona. In the American Southwest, the depletion of aquifers has threatened agriculture.

Other aquifers are drying up in California, Arizona, New Mexico, Texas, Kansas, Florida, and Long Island in New York. California has a twenty-year supply of freshwater left. In that state's San Joaquin Valley, the water table beneath the area's fertile farmlands has dropped dramatically, sinking 33 feet (10 meters) in the past fifty years.[14] New Mexico has only a ten-year supply. Arizona now imports much of its drinking water. East of Phoenix, the water table has dropped about 390 feet (119 meters).[15] This was due to groundwater withdrawal to meet the needs of agricultural production and also residential development.

In some areas of the Ogallala aquifer, there has been so much depletion of water that the land above the aquifer is sinking. This process is called subsidence. This is also a problem in Mexico City. There, the city is sinking at a rate of 20 inches (51 centimeters) a year.[16]

According to activist and author Maude Barlow:

> Anxious American politicians talk about 'drought' as if this is a cyclical situation that will right itself. But scientists and water managers throughout the American Midwest and Southwest are saying that it is more than a drought: major parts of the United States are running out of water. In fact, the Environmental Protection Agency (EPA) warns that if current water use continues unchecked, thirty-six states will suffer water shortages within the next five years.[17]

Some cities in the southeastern part of the United States, such as Atlanta, are facing severe water shortages due to rapid population growth. The problem is especially critical during times of drought. But even in years of normal rainfall, these areas are experiencing lower levels in their reservoirs.

Groundwater is continuously replenished by the hydrological cycle. But natural recharge cannot keep up with the rate of withdrawal. The water on the earth today is the same that went through the hydrological cycle millions of years ago. The water we drink is the same water that the dinosaurs drank.

So if the total amount of water on Earth has always been constant, why are we beginning to run out of freshwater? The problem is partly caused by humans mismanaging and wasting the water supply as well as polluting and poisoning this resource. Other factors are the ever-increasing numbers of people in the world and the concentration of too many people in certain areas. Each year millions of additional people require part of the total finite amount of available water. According to Allerd Stikker of the Ecological Management Foundation in Amsterdam:

> The issue today, put simply, is that while the only renewable source of freshwater is continental rainfall ... [a finite amount of water], the world population keeps increasing by roughly 85 million per year. Therefore the availability of freshwater per head is decreasing rapidly.[18]

Thinking Green About Water

The serious nature of the water crisis the world faces is going to require us to think "green" as far as water is concerned. The overall "green" effort is aimed at protecting the environment. Its goal is to help to make the world a nourishing place for all living things. Of course, thinking green about water calls upon each one of us to change our behaviors to preserve this precious resource. The concept of green water also includes the implementation of sensible policies regarding water conservation, water restoration, and the protection of water quality.

Green water means ecologically friendly policies for the management and use of freshwater supplies. Such policies have been put into practice in many parts of the world with varying degrees of success. In the United States, many programs at the federal and state levels have been created to deal with a long list of interrelated water problems in need of solutions.

CALFED is one example of an ambitious attempt by state and federal governments to address many of California's statewide water challenges. (Its name is derived from *CALifornia* and the *FEDeral* government, the two bodies participating in the program.) Established in December 1994, CALFED consists of many different groups and agencies all having something to do with water policies. These include public and private groups, and twenty-three state and federal agencies. The overall goal is to create water policies that balance the interests of three main groups—agricultural, urban, and environmental. In order to accomplish its goals,

> CALFED intends to modify 188,000 acres of wetlands and streamside habitat, establish 385,000 "wildlife-friendly" agricultural acres, recharge underground aquifers, streamline water transfers, promote water use efficiency, clean contaminated agricultural runoff, and study the feasibility of building new reservoirs and of raising dams to increase storage.[19]

In 2008, California governor Arnold Schwarzenegger proposed a $9.3 billion water bond to update the state's water system. The plan included increasing water storage, improving movement of water, protecting the ecosystem of the San Francisco Bay–Sacramento River Delta, and promoting greater water conservation. The governor's plan at first sounded like a green approach to water. It seemed to conform to CALFED's goal of balancing the needs of farmers, urban planners, and environmental advocates.

But the plan proved to be controversial, showing the difficulty of achieving a balanced approach to managing water resources. Agribusiness was pleased because the project would deliver more water from the delta to the huge farms in California's Central Valley. But a coalition of recreational fishing groups, commercial fishing organizations, American Indian tribes, and environmental groups were opposed to the plan.

The water bond proposed building a peripheral canal and two new reservoirs. But this would lead to a dramatic decline in salmon and several other species of fish.

Some environmentalists were afraid the new dams and the canal would destroy San Francisco Bay, the largest estuary on the West Coast. (An estuary is a semienclosed coastal body of water, with one or more rivers or streams flowing into it and with a free connection to the open sea. The freshwater rivers mix with seawater in the estuary.) The environmentalists saw the governor's water plan as extremely destructive of California's environment.

A lettuce farm in California. CALFED is trying to address the state's problems related to water availability and use.

On the other side of the world, water scarcity mainly affects developing countries. That is where the majority of the world's undernourished people—approximately 840 million—live. In Africa, much of the focus has been on the provision of drinking water and sanitation. These are vital goals with respect to living standards. But the provision of water for agriculture is also extremely important. There will be a need for new large and medium-sized dams to deal with the critical lack of water storage. But other, simpler, solutions, such as the construction of small reservoirs, will also play an important role.

Improved simple irrigation techniques will bring about increases in food productivity. It is possible to save a tremendous amount of water with drip irrigation. The most popular type of conventional irrigation is the sprinkler system. This system is a high-pressure, high-flow method of water delivery that gets a lot of water to the crops but also wastes water through runoff in the soil. Drip irrigation is a low-flow, low-pressure system. It involves putting water through perforated hoses that are aimed at the crops. The hoses deliver just the right amount of water and nutrients required for the crop being grown.

Ultimately, in any geographic area, all aspects of water use need to be taken into account in creating and implementing policies that preserve and protect agricultural, household, industrial, energy, and environmental uses of water.

2
······

Problems of
Water Scarcity

Imagine what it would be like to live in one of the driest places on the earth. The Atacama Desert, situated on the coast of northern Chile, is just such a place. It hardly ever rains there. Indeed, it is said that in some parts of that desert it has never rained. But fogs roll in regularly from the cold offshore current of the Pacific Ocean. Residents of the isolated towns along the coast, who rely on fishing for their survival, call the thick, moist fog the *camanchaca,* or creeping fog.

For centuries, people observed how local plants collected tiny water droplets in the fog. In the 1960s Chilean scientists came up with a way to tap this water source. They invented a system of fog-catchers, volleyball-style nets that stand upright on the hilltops. As the wind drives the fog through the nets,

The Atacama Desert of northern Chile is one of the driest
spots on Earth.

tiny droplets of water get trapped in the nets' plastic mesh. The droplets then form large drops that run down into a trough that flows to the town below.

In the late 1980s, the Chileans set up their first fog-catching project in the town of Chungungo. Previously, water for the town had to be trucked in from fifty miles away, and the town was dying. The fog-catchers provided the town an average of four thousand gallons of water a day.[1] With a secure water supply, people began to return to Chungungo. Today, fog-catching systems have been set up in many other communities along the Pacific coast of South America.

Unequal Distribution of Precipitation

According to science writer Marq de Villiers:

> The trouble with water—and there is trouble with water—is that they're not making any more of it. They're not making any less, mind, but no more either. There is the same amount of water on the planet now as there was in prehistoric times. People, however, they're making more of—many more, far more than is ecologically sensible—and all those people are utterly dependent on water for their lives (humans consist mostly of water), for their livelihoods, their food, and, increasingly, their industry. Humans can live for a month without food but will die in less than a week without water. Humans consume water,

discard it, poison it, waste it, and restlessly change the hydrological cycles, indifferent to the consequences: too many people, too little water, water in the wrong places and in the wrong amounts. The human population is burgeoning, but water demand is increasing twice as fast.[2]

According to the United Nations Population Division, "the vast majority of population growth—95 percent—is occurring in developing countries. Africa has the highest growth rate of any region: 2.4 percent annually. Its population is expected to more than double by 2050, to 2.3 billion."[3]

Some scientists estimate that we will not have enough water to feed ourselves in twenty-five years' time. There will simply not be enough water available for agriculture. They base this on the growing scarcity of freshwater supplies in many parts of the world and on the increasing global population. More and more people will create ever greater demand for the available water.

In the American Southwest, the Colorado River is already under stress from the worst drought conditions in its recorded history. Huge numbers of people from the Rust Belt states in the upper Midwest have been migrating to parched places such as Arizona and Nevada. This will only add to the crisis.

Unfortunately, precipitation and water resources are not uniformly distributed all over the globe. For example, China has less water than Canada, but forty times more people. Greenland has about 8 million gallons of water available for each of its citizens each day.[4] At the other extreme, Kuwait has to make do with only eight gallons per citizen. And while Wadi Halfa, Sudan, gets less than 0.1 inches of rain a year, Quibdo, Colombia, gets an average of 354 inches.[5]

Some parts of the world with the fastest growing populations—and therefore the greatest needs for clean, fresh water—have very low annual rainfall and are prone to severe droughts. This is true in parts of Africa, especially south of the Sahara, and in certain areas of south Asia.

A season of torrential downpours followed by one of drought is an often-repeated pattern in tropical regions. In other areas, windward slopes that receive heavy precipitation and support lush vegetation are commonly adjacent to deserts located in the mountains' rain shadow—that is, clouds drop most of their precipitation when they hit one side of the mountain range, and then the mountains act as a shield, keeping the areas on the other side dry. These deserts may go years between rains and average only a few inches per year, which may come all at once during a cloudburst.

Global Warming

Many scientists believe that global warming will only add to the problem of water scarcity by increasing evaporation rates and decreasing snow packs. They say that certain areas can expect more severe and more frequent storms, accompanied by disastrous flooding. But in other places, global warming will increase the severity of droughts due to reduced rainfall.

Global warming, the overall warming of the earth, has accelerated due to human actions. Gases that exist naturally in Earth's atmosphere in the form of water vapor, carbon dioxide, methane and other trace gases absorb radiation and trap heat in the atmosphere—much as the glass in a greenhouse traps heat—hence the name "greenhouse gases." Greenhouse gases make Earth habitable for all forms of life. By burning fossil fuels, such as oil, gas, and coal, we have increased the greenhouse gases in the upper atmosphere, thus disrupting Earth's energy balance (e.g., radiation coming in versus radiation going out). Burning of fossil fuels adds carbon dioxide to the atmosphere, which in turn strengthens the greenhouse effect. Other greenhouse gases, including methane and nitrous oxide, have been building up in the atmosphere and are also contributing to global warming. Agricultural activities and the burning of fossil fuels are responsible for the increased methane. Agriculture and the chemical industry are sources of nitrous oxide.

The Earth warmed by an average of 1°F in the last century. Scientists predict that global temperatures could increase by 2.5°F to as much as 10.5°F in the twenty-first century. Nearly all scientists agree that global warming will bring about unpredictable changes in climate that will almost certainly result in unpleasant consequences in at least some parts of the world.

According to a study by the U.S. Department of Agriculture (USDA) and the U.S. Climate Change Science Program,

> Warming is very likely to continue in the United States during the next 25 to 50 years, regardless of reductions in greenhouse gas emissions, due to emissions that have already occurred. U.S.

This NASA photo, taken in 2005, shows Arctic Sea ice, which dropped to the lowest level ever recorded.

ecosystems and natural resources are already being affected by climate system changes and variability.[6]

Elsewhere, as ice melts in the polar regions, the sea level around the world will rise. This will inundate some islands and the low coastal areas of many continents. Rising sea levels may contaminate coastal aquifers with salt water. In the arctic, the area covered year-round by sea ice is diminishing each year at an alarming rate. Scientists believe that by the year 2013, the North Polar region could be entirely free of ice during the summer months.[7]

At the other end of the earth, scientists believe that the ice of the vast West Antarctic Ice Sheet could disintegrate. This would cause sea levels around the world to rise an average of 10.83 feet (3.3 meters).[8]

Global warming will bring drastic changes in climates around the globe. As the air temperatures rise, evaporation from the oceans will increase. This process will result in storms that are more destructive. There could also be an 8 to 10 percent increase in the amount of water vapor in the atmosphere. That will cause an increase in levels of global rainfall. But these changes in the atmosphere will result in shifts in the paths of rain-producing weather systems. So rainfall patterns will change as rainfall is redistributed. Middle-latitude areas, such as the plains of the western United States, could become drier.[9]

The flows of water in individual rivers around the world will be affected by the changes in precipitation patterns and rates of evaporation. According to the best guesses of scientists, many dry areas will become drier while wet areas will become wetter. As a result, according to writer Fred Pearce,

> Many of the rivers that provide water in the world's most densely populated areas and where water is already in the shortest supply will be in still deeper trouble soon. In northeastern China, the savanna grasslands of Africa, the Mediterranean, and the southern and western coasts of Australia, rains will probably diminish, evaporation will certainly be greater—and the rivers will run dry.[10]

Global warming will affect water in yet another way resulting in increased scarcity. Mountain glaciers provide flows of water that feed into some of the world's most important rivers. According to Pearce,

> The glaciers of the Himalayas and Tibet feed seven of the greatest rivers in Asia—the Ganges, Indus, Brahmaputra, Salween, Irrawaddy, Mekong, and Yangtze—ensuring reliable water supplies for 2 billion people. But in half a century or so, the glacier flows in many of these rivers will dwindle and be replaced by much more fickle flows from rain in the mountains. That is a serious threat to Asia's future.[11]

Meanwhile in South America, cities in the Andes face a similar threat. La Paz in Bolivia, Lima in Peru, and Quito in Ecuador also depend on glaciers for their water and hydroelectric power. And the glaciers are disappearing fast.

Water Wars

Water shortages will increase the likelihood of conflicts over a scarce resource. Indeed, access to freshwater has already been a major factor in at least one war. According to Fred Pearce, the Six-Day War in 1967 between Israel and its Arab neighbors was the first modern water war. According to Pearce, Israeli leader Ariel Sharon in his autobiography described how Syria had begun digging a canal in the Golan Heights to divert the headwaters of the Jordan River away from Israel. Sharon wrote, "The Six-Day War really started on the day Israel decided to act against the diversion of the Jordan…. While the border disputes were of great significance, the matter of water diversion was a stark issue of life and death."[12]

But three years earlier, in 1964, Israel, without the agreement of Syria or Jordan, had begun pumping water out of the Jordan River. This would eventually deprive Israel's neighbors of the Jordan's waters. For thousands of years, the Jordan River had flowed from the Golan Heights down into the Sea of Galilee, eventually reaching the Dead Sea at the lower end of the Jordan Valley. But Israel constructed a dam, preventing the

Women on the outskirts of Hyderabad, Pakistan, go to a nearby well to collect water. Pakistan has a shortage of clean drinking water, a situation that could lead to international conflict.

Jordan from flowing beyond the Sea of Galilee. A huge pipe, known as the National Water Carrier, was built to lift water 1200 feet (366 meters) out of the valley. Israel now depended on the Water Carrier to supply most of its water. By 1991, no freshwater flowed out of the Sea of Galilee into the lower Jordan Valley.

In many other parts of the world, disputes over access to water may be setting the stage for future conflicts. In some of these situations, a river forms the boundary between two or more countries. In others, a country through which a river flows may build dams, preventing the waters from reaching the nations downstream. The possibilities for trouble become clear when you consider that the Danube and Rhine in Europe and the Niger and Congo in Africa each pass through nine countries. The Zambezi in Africa flows through eight countries. In most of these places, there are no treaties for sharing water.

A particularly dangerous source of potential conflict over water exists between India and Pakistan. The two nuclear-armed nations have already fought three wars. The first began when India cut the flow of tributaries of the Indus River in Kashmir—water Pakistan relied on. In 1960, both countries signed the Indus Waters Treaty, obliging them to share the flow of the Indus River. Each nation was to take water from three tributaries of the Indus. But India is building a dam on the Chenab River, one of the tributaries. India claims the purpose of the dam is to provide hydroelectric power, and that water will still flow to Pakistan. But Pakistan fears that in a future crisis, India could cut off the flow of the Chenab—with disastrous results for Pakistan. So

Water shortages will increase the likelihood of conflicts over a scarce resource.

Pakistan views the dam, known as the Baglihar barrage, as a dangerous breach of the Indus Waters Treaty.

In Africa, the Nile flows northward through ten countries, including Ethiopia, Sudan, Egypt, Uganda, Kenya, Tanzania, Burundi, Rwanda, the Democratic Republic of Congo, and Eritrea. At the downstream end lies Egypt, which gets 97 percent of its water from its upstream neighbors. The current water treaty dates from the days when Great Britain ruled the region. It grants most of the Nile's flow to Egypt. Some of the Nile's waters are for Sudan. But none are allocated for Ethiopia or any of the other countries upstream. In a part of the world that receives almost no rainfall, the Nile is obviously an extremely vital resource. Someday, one of the countries through which the Nile flows may decide it absolutely must have some of that water. But Egypt has warned that it would go to war if any of the upstream countries, such as Ethiopia, starts diverting the Nile's water.

The Tigris and Euphrates rivers are the major water bodies sustaining agriculture for thousands of years in Turkey, Syria, and Iraq. Water development projects on the Euphrates have been the cause of armed conflict between Turkey, Syria, Iraq, and the Kurds. The construction of the Ataturk Dam (1983–1990) on the Euphrates in Turkey led to feuding with Iraq. Water bound for Iraq was diverted to southern Turkey by a tunnel from the dam. The completion of new dams in Turkey will result in Iraq's losing 80 to 90 percent of its allotment of

Euphrates water. And the conflict between the two countries is expected to intensify.

Many other water hot spots exist between nations and even within nations. In southern India, the Cauvery River has been the source of a feud between Karnataka and Tamil Nadu. The two states have been arguing for decades over water rights.

In the American Southwest, the states in the region all have claims on the waters of the Colorado River. The Colorado is a totally managed system with more than twenty dams along its 1,470-mile (2,365-kilometer) length. The largest of these are Hoover Dam and Glen Canyon Dam. Water from Lake Havasu (Parker Dam) is transferred to California through an aqueduct running 242 miles (389 kilometers) from the Colorado River. California accounts for just 1.6 percent of the 242,000-square-mile (626,780 square-kilometer) Colorado basin.[13] But although it inputs nothing to the river, California uses one-fourth of the Colorado River's water. The management of the Colorado River made phenomenal growth possible in Southern California. But it is estimated that evaporation causes the loss of one cubic mile of water from Lake Havasu each year. By the time the Colorado River reaches Mexico, there is barely a drop of water left. Naturally, Mexico—which was supposed to get 1.5 million acre-feet by treaty—is not pleased. (One acre-foot of water is equal to 325,851 gallons. This is the amount of water required to cover an area of one acre to a depth of one foot.)

In 1869, Major John Wesley Powell made a voyage of exploration along the Colorado River. He explored the Grand Canyon, the immense gash in the earth carved by the river. Powell saw that the Colorado could provide enough water to sustain future development of the region. But he was aware that there were limits to making the desert bloom. In 1893, he said, "I wish to make it clear to you, there is not sufficient water to irrigate all the lands which could be irrigated, and only a small portion can be irrigated.... I tell you, gentlemen, you are piling up a heritage of conflict."[14]

By the late 1890s, the rapidly growing city of Los Angeles needed new sources of water to provide for further development. The city secretly bought land and water rights in the Owens Valley, a couple of hundred miles to the north. Writer Vandana Shiva notes:

> This clandestine agreement to transfer water from the farms to the city led to intense conflict between Owens Valley residents and Los Angeles water users.... In 1924, Owens Valley residents blasted an aqueduct to prevent water diversion to Los Angeles. The water war had begun. After 12 more blasts, armed guards were stationed on the aqueduct with orders to kill.... During the drought of 1929, groundwater pumping began but quickly dried up the 75-square mile Owens Lake. New scarcity had bred new conflicts. In 1976, the aqueduct was bombed again.[15]

Recently it has occurred to managers of water resources that dams make tempting targets for would-be terrorists. In September 2004, the Chinese military responded to rumors of a terrorist attack on the Three Gorges Dam on the Yangtze River. Three Gorges, completed in 2007, is the world's largest hydroelectric dam. Some 10 million people who had been living in the Yangtze River Valley were displaced by construction of the dam. The giant dam holds back a reservoir 300 miles (483 kilometers) long. The reservoir contains 32 million acre-feet of water. If the dam were to be destroyed, the water would sweep downstream, most likely creating the worst man-made disaster in history.[16]

The privatization of water resources is creating yet another type of water conflict. Around the globe, major corporations seek to control and profit from the sale of water. Among the biggest players are the French companies Vivendi Environment and Suez Lyonnaise des Eaux, the Spanish company Aguas de Barcelona, and the British companies Thames Water, Biwater, and United Utilities. Arguments for privatization are based on the poor performance of public water utilities. The World Bank and the International Monetary Fund, or IMF, have provided funding for privatization projects, known as "public-private partnerships." The name is misleading, because it suggests public participation, democracy, and accountability. But in reality, such projects usually mean that public funds are made available for the privatization of public goods, such as water.

Three Gorges Dam on the Yangtze River in China, the world's largest hydroelectric dam. The Chinese government is concerned about the possibility of a terrorist attack on the dam.

Such projects often lack accountability, have poor track records, and result in price gouging.

According to Vandana Shiva:

> In Chile, Suez Lyonnaise des Eaux insisted on a 35 percent profit. In Casablanca, consumers saw the price of water increase threefold. In Britain, water and sewage bills increased 67 percent between 1989-90 and 1994-95. The rate at which people's services were disconnected rose by 177 percent. In New Zealand, citizens took to the

streets to protest the commercialization of water. In South Africa, Johannesburg's water supply was overtaken by Suez Lyonnaise des Eaux. Water soon became unsafe, inaccessible, and unafford-able. Thousands of people were disconnected and cholera infections became rampant.[17]

In April 2000, the people of Cochabamba, Bolivia, won a victory against the powerful Bechtel Corporation. The year before, the World Bank had recommended privatization. The government of Bolivia then passed a drinking water and sanitation law, allowing privatization of the water utility. Bechtel stepped in. Unfortunately for the residents of Cochabamba—many of whom earned less than sixty dollars a month—water bills skyrocketed. With charges of twenty dollars a month, most people could not afford water. Twenty dollars was the cost of feeding the average family of five for two weeks.[18]

The citizens of Cochabamba formed an alliance called the Coalition in Defense of Water and Life. They held mass pro-tests and a general strike. In their Cochabamba Declaration, the protesters stated that the water rights of every citizen must be protected. They demanded that the government repeal the drinking water law. The government refused. Protests contin-ued, with thousands of marchers using slogans such as "Water Is Life" and "Water Is God's Gift and Not a Merchandise." Activists were arrested, protesters killed, and the media cen-sored. Finally, the government had had enough. On April 10,

2000, it issued an order for Bechtel to leave the country. The citizens of Cochabamba had proved that corporate takeover of water supplies could be prevented by the democratic will of the people.

Solutions to Water Scarcity

Faced with shortages of freshwater, communities in various parts of the world have tried a number of different strategies for supplying the much-needed water. Rain harvesting was once a worldwide technology on which hundreds of millions of people depended. Today, all across India, groups are harvesting the rain either for direct use or to revive underground water reserves. Scattered across the country are about one hundred forty thousand tanks. Most of these are shallow mud-walled reservoirs in valley bottoms. They cover a couple of acres at most and can irrigate up to fifty acres. As farmers are having to pump from ever greater depths to retrieve underground water, the old tanks are starting to be restored.

Some 2 million people in the desolate Gansu region of western China also get most of their water for drinking and growing crops by harvesting rain. They collect rainwater in bell-shaped cisterns. The cisterns can hold about sixteen thousand gallons (sixty-one thousand liters) of water. Every household in the region has one cistern.

Elsewhere, people have resorted to a more ancient method of making rain. According to Fred Pearce:

> Some have even suggested using sound to capture moisture from the air. On a cool, still night, the air can be so saturated with moisture that modest air movements, such as sound waves, can condense the moisture and produce raindrops. In the mountains of Yunan in southern China, villagers have a tradition of yelling loudly in the hope that it will stimulate rain. The louder they shout, it is said, the more it rains. This gives interesting scientific credence to the African notion of the rain dance, once seen as the epitome of superstition.[19]

Another approach involves the use of purification systems for recycling wastewater. Wastewater has been used in many places for agriculture. Now, increasingly, recycled wastewater is being promoted as perfectly safe for cooking and drinking. Such wastewater can be a good source of water for industrial use in the workplace or garden, toilets, and cleaning in the home. But there are real concerns about bathing, drinking, or cooking with recycled water. Treated water has often been found to contain many toxic substances. According to U.S. cancer expert Dr. Steven Oppenheimer, "the 'toilet to tap' process should only be considered as a last resort."[20] At current treatment levels, Oppenheimer compared drinking recycled water to playing "Russian roulette" with human life.

Cloud Seeding

Some people believe that seeding the clouds to make rain can solve the water crisis. Scientists fly a plane into the clouds and spray billions of silver iodide crystals into the clouds. The tiny particles become the nuclei around which water droplets form and become raindrops. At least ten American states, from Texas to North Dakota, and twenty-four countries around the world currently practice cloud seeding. All claim varying degrees of success. But how could you scientifically prove that any rain that falls would not have fallen anyway without the cloud seeding?

Assuming that cloud seeding works, there could still be problems. Suppose you were to succeed in condensing enough water above a particular area to produce precipitation. You would be depriving locations downwind from receiving rain. This could heighten political tensions. For example, Israel has claimed great success with its cloud-seeding programs. According to the Israelis, spraying the winter clouds over the hills of Galilee raises rainfall by 15 percent and produces forty thousand acre-feet of water a year. But the Israelis may be harvesting water that would have crossed the Jordan Valley into Jordan.[21]

What about the oceans as a source of water? After all, the oceans contain most of the earth's water. Sometimes oceans are considered to be available water, but what about all the salt? Is desalination a solution to water scarcity? The possibility of converting an unlimited quantity of seawater to freshwater certainly seems a promising solution. But the amount of energy needed to convert salt water to drinkable freshwater is costly. A very small fraction of the world's water supply currently comes from desalination. Nevertheless, as the global water crisis grows worse, managers of water resources are increasingly looking to desalination as the answer to their problems.

Desalination is actually a very old technology. It involved distilling seawater by boiling it and collecting the water vapor. In the fourth century B.C., the Greek philosopher Aristotle wrote that "saltwater, when it turns into vapor, becomes sweet and the vapor does not form saltwater again when it condenses."[22]

President John F. Kennedy strongly believed in the importance of desalination. In a speech in June 1961, he said:

> Before this decade is out we will see more and more evidence of man's ability at an economic rate to secure freshwater from saltwater, and when that day comes, then we will literally see the deserts bloom. This is a work ... more important than any other scientific enterprise in which this country is now engaged.... It can do more to raise men and women from lives of poverty than any other scientific advance.[23]

A worker at a desalination project on the Rio Grande in Texas holds two containers of water. On the right is untreated seawater; on the left is treated water with the salt removed.

There are now twenty-one thousand desalination plants worldwide in 120 countries. These plants produce a combined total of 3 billion gallons (11 billion liters) of drinking water a day. Most of these plants are small. In oil-rich Saudi Arabia, there are two thousand desalination plants, making up one-quarter of the world's desalinated water production. Eventually, all of Saudi Arabia's freshwater will come from desalinated seawater. Saudi Arabia, Israel, and other Middle Eastern countries, as well as certain Caribbean islands, are among the few places where desalination provides a substantial portion of the water supply. The International Desalination Association predicts that demand around the world for desalinated water will grow by about 25 percent a year. Israel, Singapore, and Australia are just three of the countries in which large desalination plants are currently being built. More than a dozen large-scale ocean desalination plants are being planned in California. One of these, just north of San Diego, will be the largest of its kind in the Western Hemisphere. It will provide enough water for three hundred thousand people.

During the Second World War, the U.S. Navy developed a modern distillation technology to provide freshwater on remote Pacific islands. Today, distillation is still being used in about four fifths of the world's desalination plants. But another technology, known as reverse osmosis, has grown in popularity since the 1970s.

There are two methods of reverse osmosis. In one, seawater is forced through a membrane. The membrane is semipermeable. As the seawater passes through the membrane, the salt molecules in the water are filtered out by the membrane. So the water passing through the membrane has become freshwater. In the other type of reverse osmosis, salt ions in the water are moved through the membrane by electrical currents. The water left behind has become freshwater. This process is known as electrodialysis. Both methods rely on very sophisticated membranes, specially developed for the reverse osmosis process. Unfortunately, desalination technologies require huge amounts of energy. Most of the energy comes from burning coal, oil, and other fossil fuels. And energy derived from fossil fuels uses water to produce it. So not only does desalinated water cost about a hundred times more than conventional water in most places, but the technology used to produce it emits greenhouse gases that contribute to global warming.

On the horizon, the use of alternative types of energy promises to address these problems. According to Leon Awerbuch of the Bechtel Corporation, "In the long run, sustainable [desalination] development requires us to look at renewable sources like solar energy and its derivatives, wind, ocean thermal, waves, and alternative energy like nuclear, because of limits of supply of fossil fuel and the potential impact of [the] greenhouse effect."[24] The International Atomic Energy Agency is enthusiastically promoting the use of nuclear reactors as the source of energy for desalination.

But there are other serious environmental problems with desalination. All desalination plants have to dispose of a huge stream of concentrated brine. This is what remains when the salt is extracted from the seawater. The desalination plants also

> **One large-scale desalination plant in California will provide enough water for 300,000 people.**

have to get rid of various chemicals and heavy metals. These substances are used to clean and maintain the reverse osmosis membranes and to prevent salt erosion. The chemicals and metals are mixed with the brine. Most desalination plants pump this lethal mixture back into the sea, polluting the nearby waters. And in countries that discharge their waste into the ocean, much of the water available to an offshore desalination plant is polluted.

There are yet other problems. Environmentalists are concerned that widespread adoption of desalination technologies may lead people to believe that freshwater is no longer scarce, because there is no danger of the oceans running out of water. Also, desalination plants close to coral reefs in warm tropical seas could cause harm to these important ecosystems. And coral reefs, according to writer Jeffrey Rothfeder, "provide habitat and nutrients for about four thousand species of fish, many of which feed a large part of the world's population—one billion people in Asia alone."[25] Even so, to many, desalination appears to be an excellent technology fix. Many factors should be weighed before desalination is adopted as a water source.

3

Water Pollution

In 1997, Charles Moore, an ocean researcher, was sailing through an area of the Pacific Ocean known as the North Pacific Subtropical Gyre. The area lies about 1,000 miles (1,609 kilometers) west of California and an equal distance north of Hawaii. Circular winds over this vast expanse of sea produce circular ocean currents that spiral into a center where there is a slight down-welling.

Moore and his crew made an astounding discovery:

> There were shampoo caps and soap bottles and plastic bags and fishing floats as far as I could see. Here I was in the middle of the ocean, and there was nowhere I could go to avoid the plastic. It seemed unbelievable, but I never found a clear

spot. In the week it took to cross, no matter what time of day I looked, plastic debris was floating everywhere.[1]

Moore continues to research the area, which oceanographers now refer to as the Great Pacific Garbage Patch, or the Eastern Garbage Patch. According to Moore, the patch may cover an area as much as one and a half times the size of the United States. The rubbish, which extends to a depth of 100 feet (30 meters) and more in some places, drifts—sometimes as far as the Hawaiian Islands. When that occurs, Waimanalo Beach on Oahu gets coated with blue-green plastic sand.

The floating pieces of plastic are not biodegradable. But they are broken down by sunshine, wind, and waves into smaller and smaller pieces. The pieces of plastic polymers eventually become individual molecules of plastic. No matter how small the particles, they cannot be digested by any organism. But they are ingested by many kinds of sea life. The polymer particles also absorb oily toxins in the water, such as DDT and PCBs. These poisons eventually work their way into the food chain. They move up from small marine organisms to fish and into the food we eat. Moore has discovered other areas of floating trash outside the patch. Indeed, according to Moore, it is now possible that *all* food in the ocean contains plastic.

It has taken about sixty years for the Great Pacific Garbage Patch to develop. It began in the years after World War II,

This jar holds pieces of plastic from the Great Pacific Garbage Patch—plastic that will never biodegrade.

when production of plastics skyrocketed. According to Moore, it takes several years for a piece of plastic to get to the patch from the United States, and about a year from Asia. There is another garbage patch, the Western Garbage Patch, off the coast of Japan. And there is a garbage patch in the Indian Ocean. The only way to prevent further growth of the garbage patches is to prevent more debris from entering the ocean. Without changing our habits, the garbage patches will only continue to grow. According to Moore, "We humans have got to change the way we produce and consume plastics. And then we have got to hope the ocean can clean itself up in hundreds of years."[2]

Sources of Water Pollution

As available supplies of clean freshwater become scarcer around the world, pollution becomes an increasingly serious problem. Water pollution has many causes and characteristics. Our nation's waters in many places have been polluted by either organic or inorganic substances. Sometimes both types of pollutants occur in the same place. The most common sources of water pollution are toxic substances discharged by industries in their wastewater. Organic waste such as untreated sewage also occurs in some places.

Every day a long list of contaminants enters the nation's waters. Pollution is being introduced, not only in lakes, rivers, and streams, but also in groundwater and along seacoasts. For example, giant fields of algae are floating on parts of Lake Erie. The blooms of algae, toxic to fish and small animals, can also be a health hazard to humans. According to Tom Bridgeman, a professor of environmental science, the algae is "now blossoming in the proportions that it was in the bad old days of the 1960s and early '70s. There's a mystery to it because the lake seemed to be getting cleaner, but now the algal blooms are worse."[3] Researchers say that the problem can be traced to phosphorus from suburban development along the lakeshore. The thick algae, fed by the phosphorus, gives off bad smells. Local water utilities have to spend thousands of dollars a day to kill the algae.

The Great Pacific Garbage Patch may cover an area as much as one and a half times the size of the United States.

Pollution that can be traced to a single source is known as point source pollution. This includes sources such as an underground storage tank, an irrigation ditch, or a pipe discharging into a river or stream. Often a body of water is affected by several or many different sources of pollution. These sources may be industrial or agricultural. The pollution in such a case is referred to as nonpoint source pollution. In both types of pollution, the sources may be organic or inorganic.

Organic water pollutants come from many types of sources. Pathogens—disease-causing organisms such as bacteria,

This humpback whale became entangled in plastic line and had a buoy lodged in its mouth. Wildlife scientists were able to remove the debris from the whale, but most marine animals are not so lucky.

parasites, or viruses—enter water systems through infected raw sewage or animal wastes. Organic chemical pollutants include wastes from petroleum refineries, chemical factories, and from canning, meat-packing, and food-processing plants. Runoff from farmlands contains large amounts of organic pesticides and fertilizers. There are also many synthetic organic pollutants, such as gasoline, oils, plastics, solvents, and wood preservatives.

There are also many types of inorganic water pollutants, including inorganic chemicals such as acids, salts, and heavy metals; and certain fertilizers, including nitrates and phosphates. Heavy metals include mercury, lead, cadmium, arsenic, nickel, and chromium. Heavy metal compounds are often by-products of industrial processes such as metal treatment and paint and plastics production. Acids, heavy metal, and heavy metal compounds enter water systems as a result of seepage, runoff, and direct discharge by factories.

Groundwater Pollution

All bodies of water can become polluted. Even the water in underground aquifers is not safe from contamination. At one time, it was believed that the soil above an aquifer would filter out any pollutants. It is true that soils may absorb toxic substances. And the vegetation and bacteria in some soils will neutralize some contaminants. But a sudden leak or spill from a tank of gasoline can overload the soil's capacity to filter substances that

Factory Farms

Factory farms are giant livestock farms that house thousands of cows, pigs, or chickens. These farms are also known as feedlots or concentrated animal feeding operations (CAFOs). Factory farms in the United States produce staggering amounts of animal waste, as much as 500 million tons per year.

Too many farm animals confined in a single facility create an environmental mess. Their manure and urine are funneled into huge waste lagoons, which can leak into rivers, streams, and groundwater and contaminate drinking water. According to the EPA, pollution from farm animal wastes is very widespread. About 35,000 miles of rivers in twenty-two states have been polluted by hog, chicken, and cattle waste. And groundwater has been contaminated in seventeen states.[4]

The waste from factory farm animals contains nitrates, nitrogen, phosphorus, and dangerous microbes, including drug-resistant bacteria. Because the health of the animals can be adversely affected by the crowded conditions, factory farms give their animals antibiotics to prevent illness and to promote growth. This contributes to the rise of antibiotic-resistant bacteria, which makes it harder to treat human diseases.

Until the government regulates factory farm practices, there are things we can do to help stop factory farm pollution. When shopping in the grocery store, check meat labels for "organic," "free range," "antibiotic-free," or similar wording. This indicates that the meat has been raised in a more sustainable and "green" manner.

might pollute groundwater. And pollutants in groundwater can be transported great distances as the water moves through pore space, cracks, and caverns in unseen aquifers.

Leakage from underground gasoline storage tanks makes up an estimated 40 percent of all groundwater contamination. There are 1.4 million underground tanks in the United States. And 5 to 10 percent of these tanks are believed to be leaking. One or two drips per second of gasoline seeping out of an

Pigs on a farm in Arkansas. Such farms produce enormous amounts of animal waste, creating huge environmental problems.

underground tank can seriously pollute an aquifer, given enough time. Such a leak will release about one gallon (3.8 liters) of gas per day, more than 350 gallons (1,325 liters) in a year. This rate of leakage can pollute the water supply of tens of thousands of people. Such a leak can be hard to detect, because losses are so slow they usually go unnoticed.

Human waste and toxic chemicals dumped into sewage systems are probably the greatest threats to groundwater quality and human health. Approximately 20 million septic tanks, cesspools, and outhouses, known as on-site sewage disposal systems, are in use in at least thirty-six states, mainly in the rural areas. Pathogens, such as viruses and bacteria, may escape from septic systems through a process known as leaching. The pathogens seep through soil to groundwater. Toxic substances that have been poured down drains or that seep into groundwater from septic tanks can be health hazards also.

Dead Zones

Most water pollutants are eventually carried by rivers into the oceans. When the Mississippi River flows toward the Gulf of Mexico, it carries pollutants. These have a deadly effect when the river's waters empty into the gulf. Upstream, nitrogen and phosphorus from farmers' fields seep into the river. Farmers use nitrogen and phosphorus to fertilize their crops. The Mississippi carries an estimated 1.5 million metric tons of nitrogen and phosphorus pollution into the gulf every year.

In the Gulf of Mexico, the nitrogen and phosphorus fertilize algae in the water. The algae is eaten by microscopic animals called zooplankton. After feeding on the algae, the zooplankton excrete pellets that sink to the bottom like tiny stones. As this organic matter decays, it depletes the water of oxygen. This creates a "dead zone," a condition known as hypoxia, where there is too little oxygen to support fish, shrimp, crabs, and other forms of marine life. Fishermen have to look elsewhere for their livelihood, usually farther out in the gulf.

Scientists began to study the dead zone in the Gulf of Mexico in the 1980s. It varies in size each year. The largest dead zone occurred in 2002, when it measured nearly 8,500 square miles (22,000 square kilometers). During years when the Mississippi floods, the dead zone grows larger, because a greater amount of fertilizers wash downstream. In 2008, after record floods, the dead zone again expanded to near-record size of about eight thousand square miles (twenty-one thousand square kilometers). In 2009, the dead zone was 3,000 square miles (7,770 square kilometers), much smaller than the predicted 7,450–8,450 square miles (19,296–21,886 square kilometers). This was due to unusual weather patterns that re-oxygenated the waters.[5]

In recent years, farmers have increased their production of corn, a crop that requires extra fertilizer. The additional nitrogen in the water from record corn harvests also contributes to growth of the dead zone. And the entire Mississippi watershed, not just the gulf, is suffering the effects of agricultural runoff. About half the streams and rivers in the watershed are unsafe for swimming or for use as drinking water.

The Gulf of Mexico dead zone extends east to west along the Louisiana and Texas coasts, starting near the mouth of the Mississippi. The dead zone in the gulf is not the only one, unfortunately. Dead zones also occur in Asia, Europe, Africa, and South America. They have been reported in Chesapeake Bay, Samish Bay of Puget Sound, and Yaquina Bay in Oregon. They have also been seen in Taiwan, northern Spain, some fjords in Norway, New Zealand, and off the mouth of the Yangtze River in China. Since the 1960s, twice as many dead zones have been reported with each passing decade.

Global warming could be making the problem worse. Various parts of the world will experience heavier rains. The additional water could result in more dead zones, as more nutrients from farmlands are washed into rivers and then the sea.

Oil Spills

Pollution of the oceans by about 1 billion gallons (3.8 billion liters) of oil is an annual occurrence. Nearly half of the oil in the ocean is naturally occurring seepage from the ocean floor. The other half comes from oil tankers, offshore oil facilities, and runoff from our roads and factories by way of rivers that empty into the sea.

An offshore oil platform has an average twenty-year period of production. During this time, it can be expected to have from one to three major spills, at least twenty-five medium spills, and about two thousand small spills. A blowout, which results in a very large spill, occurs when extreme pressure explodes an offshore oil rig.

The oil industry has a long history of blowouts on offshore oil rigs and disastrous spills from oil tankers. Such events have caused enormous environmental devastation. Among the most catastrophic events were the 1969 Santa Barbara oil spill and the 1989 *Exxon Valdez* oil spill in Alaska.

In 1969, an estimated eighty thousand to one hundred thousand barrels of crude oil spilled into the Santa Barbara Channel and onto the beaches of Santa Barbara County in Southern California. The source of the oil was a blowout on Union Oil's Platform A six miles offshore.

In 1989, the oil tanker *Exxon Valdez* ran aground in Alaska's Prince William Sound. Eleven million gallons of oil spilled from the tanker. It is estimated that 350,000 birds died, as well as killer whales, dolphins, seals, otters, fish, and sea grasses along a 1,000-mile (1,609-kilometer) coastline. It took the local fishing industry years to recover.

Because an oil supertanker carries millions of gallons of crude oil, any accident is potentially disastrous. There are various causes of accidents. These include dangerous weather conditions, human error, reliance on faulty instrumentation, the use of substandard ships, and poor maintenance procedures. Although it is now illegal, some oil tankers still wash out their tanks and dump oily ballast water back into the ocean while at sea or even in port.

When an oil slick on the surface of the ocean begins to break up, oil droplets sink to the bottom of the ocean. As the

Birds soaked in oil from the *Exxon Valdez* accident. It is estimated that 350,00 birds died following the oil spill, along with whales, dolphins, otters, fish, and other animals.

droplets descend, they can clog the gills of fish and poison other sea life. Oil pollution is also a major factor in the deterioration of the world's coral reefs and mangrove swamps.

Various methods are used in attempts to clean up oil slicks. Booms and mechanical devices, also known as slick-lickers, are used to contain a spill by surrounding it with a floating barrier. Oil is then removed from the surface of the water by mechanical means. Chemical dispersants, also known as detergents, act by breaking down oil slicks into minute droplets of oil, which then disperse. Aerial spraying of chemicals is also sometimes used. The chemicals introduce new toxins into the sea. Many environmentalists believe the cleanup methods may actually do more harm than the oil itself. It seems as if major polluting of the oceans by oil will only stop when the world ends its reliance on oil as its major source of energy.

Acid Rain

Acid rain forms when large amounts of the chemicals sulfur dioxide and nitrogen oxide enter the atmosphere. The chemicals combine with water vapor, sunlight, and oxygen to produce strong acids—sulfuric acid and nitric acid. The air containing the acids cools as it rises. Then the acidic moisture turns to liquid and the resulting drops of water fall as acid rain.

Most of the chemical pollution causing acid rain comes from industrial processes, especially sulfur dioxide from power plants and smelters. Another major pollutant is nitrogen oxide from the exhaust pipes of automobiles. Winds in the atmosphere often carry clouds of acidic moisture far from the sources of the pollution, sometimes many hundreds of miles, before acid rain falls. This rain may be as much as forty times as acidic as normal rainwater.

Acid rain was first studied seriously in Sweden in the 1960s. Since then, lifeless lakes and rivers resulting from acid rain have been documented in nearly every country in the world. Rain falling on the Catskill Mountains in upstate New York is ten to twenty times as acidic as normal. The area is downwind from numerous sources of acid, mainly sulfur dioxide from coal-burning power plants in the Midwest. The high acidity in New York City's reservoirs, fed in part by water from the Catskills, may be speeding up the deterioration of those reservoirs and supply pipes. The acidity could be leaching additional toxic materials into the water.

According to writer Geoffrey C. Saign,

> The U.S. Environmental Protection Agency's National Acid Precipitation Project concluded that 10 percent of Appalachian streams are acidic; out of thousands of studied lakes and streams across the nation, 75 percent of the lakes and 47 percent of the streams were found to be acidic. In the Adirondack Mountains, 25 percent of the lakes, streams, and ponds are already too acidic to support fish life. In more than 300 such lakes all

fish have already died. In 1993, Massachusetts and Virginia experienced the highest level of stream and lake acidification since 1983, probably because of heavy acidic snow melt. Sulfate levels have decreased in some areas in the eastern United States in the past decades, thanks mainly to power plant pollution control; nitrogen levels have only leveled off.[6]

At least two steps have been taken to reduce the destructive effects of acid rain. One step involves installing what are known as "wet scrubbers" on smokestacks at coal- and oil-burning power plants, as well as at ore smelters. Scrubbers remove sulfur dioxide from smokestack emissions. The other step is the mandating of catalytic converters on all new cars. The converters reduce nitrogen oxide emissions by 60 percent and carbon monoxide and hydrocarbon emissions by 85 percent. Catalytic converters must be used with unleaded gasoline.

4
· · · · · · ·

Water Quality
and
Public Health

The town of Woburn, Massachusetts, is located just twelve miles (nineteen kilometers) northwest of Boston. In 1979, it was discovered that two wells drilled in 1964 by the local water utility were polluted with two industrial solvents. The chemicals trichloroethylene (TCE) and perchloroethylene (PCE) both cause cancer in animals. They are also believed to cause cancer in humans, as well as damage to the heart and circulatory systems, disorders of the immune and central nervous systems, and reproductive problems. Those at greatest risk from contaminants are small children, babies, and fetuses. Their rapid growth and low resistance to toxins makes them especially vulnerable.

Patricia and Kevin Kane of Woburn with lawyer Jan Schlichtmann (on left). The Kanes joined other families to sue W. R. Grace, the company that had polluted their drinking water.

Although the wells were shut down as soon as the problem became known, the damage had already been done. The local residents had been drinking water they assumed to be pure and safe. Indeed, how would they have known that W. R. Grace and Company, a manufacturer of food-processing machinery, had been polluting their wells? For years, W. R. Grace had allowed its employees to dump solvents down storm sewers. The chemicals, used to clean machine parts, had caused contamination of the aquifer beneath Woburn.

Eight Woburn families sued W. R. Grace, claiming that the company's actions had caused six leukemia deaths, heart disease, damage to the central nervous and immune systems, and many other illnesses. The jury in the trial found W. R. Grace guilty of dumping the toxic materials.

Hidden Dangers

According to writer Marq de Villiers, "Pollution leads to disease, a straight-line computation that is self-evident. Best guesses are that some 250 million new cases of waterborne diseases occur every year, killing somewhere around 10-million people—as if all of Canada were wiped out every three years."[1]

Perhaps the most famous case of toxic waste contaminants involves Love Canal, a neighborhood near Niagara Falls in upstate New York. The Love Canal neighborhood was built on an area that in the 1930s and 1940s had been used by

Hooker Chemical Company to dump toxic chemical wastes. The canal was thought to be the perfect place to dispose of the wastes. Among these wastes was dioxin, one of the most toxic substances ever created. In 1953, a layer of clay and then soil was used to cover the wastes and fill the canal. The property was sold to the local board of education, which built a school on the site. A community of new homes was built near the covered waste dump.

Waterborne diseases kill about 10 million people yearly, as if all of Canada were wiped out every three years.

Sadly, the residents of the new Love Canal neighborhood knew nothing about the toxic wastes buried beneath their homes and school. In 1976, residents noticed that water was leaking into their basements. The water contained deadly chemicals. The toxic substances dissolved tree roots and killed vegetation. By 1979, the local residents, who had been complaining about numerous health problems, realized that contamination from the dump was to blame. Among the health problems were miscarriages, birth defects, blood disease, epilepsy, hyperactivity, and cancer. President Jimmy Carter declared Love Canal a federal disaster area and provided government funding for the relocation of Love Canal families.

Unfortunately, Love Canal is by no means the only toxic waste disposal site. According to the Environmental Protection

Agency, there are at least another 180,000 toxic waste dumps across the nation. Many of these were established before there was widespread knowledge about the dangers to groundwater. The disposal sites were located over usable aquifers. This makes them a potential serious threat to drinkable water.

According to writer Steve Coffel, "New waste sites are discovered literally every day, typically only after health effects from the toxins escaping from the dumps alert residents of the area to the problem. The only difference between Love Canal and the innumerable other toxic waste sites around the country is that the extent of the damage from the chemicals leaking from the old canal is known."[2]

Waterborne Disease

In 2004, slightly more than half of the world's population, or about 3.5 billion people, had water from a safe water supply piped into their homes. Another 1.3 billion people had other ways of accessing safe water. They used water form protected springs and wells or from water kiosks. People in these two groups were the lucky ones. At least another 1 billion people led a precarious existence. With no access to a safe supply of water, they had to fetch water from unprotected wells, springs, lakes, canals, or rivers.

The lack of access to proper sanitation has led to massive outbreaks of waterborne diseases. These include diarrheal diseases, typhoid, and cholera. They are among the leading causes of illness and death in developing countries. According to Maude Barlow:

> Half of the world's hospital beds are occupied by people with an easily preventable waterborne disease, and the World Health Organization reports that contaminated water is implicated in 80 percent of all sickness and disease worldwide. In the last decade, the number of children killed by diarrhea exceeded the number of people killed in all armed conflicts since the Second World War. Every eight seconds, a child dies from drinking dirty water.[3]

Freshwater in many parts of the world may be growing scarce. But safe, clean freshwater is in extremely short supply, especially in the developing world. A glance around the world reveals some truly frightening statistics. According to the World Health Organization, more than half of China's 1.3 billion people do not have access to safe, clean water. Indeed, 700 million Chinese drink water that fails to meet the most basic standards of safety. The situation in India is even worse. More than 700 million Indians, or two thirds of the population, do not have safe water for drinking, bathing, and washing dishes. Each year, 2.1 million Indian children under age five

Martin Mhizha of Zimbabwe fetches water from an unprotected source. An outbreak of cholera in that country is linked to unsafe water supplies.

die from dirty water. In Bangladesh, almost 65 percent of the groundwater is contaminated. Because of arsenic in the groundwater, at least 1.2 million citizens of Bangladesh are exposed to arsenic. And arsenic poisoning is behind many instances of ill health, including a rising number of cancer cases.[4]

Latin America is another part of the world with major water problems. As many as 130 million people have no access to safe drinking water. Hardly any of Latin America's wastewater, as little as 2 percent, is treated in any way. In Africa, more than one-third of the population lacks access to safe drinking water. In 2006, thousands of Angolans died in a cholera outbreak. The disease was caused by filthy water.[5]

Because of the widespread pollution of surface waters in poor countries, sewage water is increasingly being used to fertil- ize crops. Wastewater agriculture seems to be a mixed blessing. It enables many poor people to earn a living and provides food supplies for the cities. However, it brings health risks as well, especially for those who eat uncooked vegetables.

In 2004, a global survey of the hidden practice of wastewa- ter irrigation was carried out by the Sri Lankan Bureau of the International Water Management Institute. According to the survey, as reported by Maude Barlow:

> One-tenth of the world's irrigated crops—from lettuce and tomatoes to mangoes and coconuts— is watered by sewage, most of it completely untreated, "gushing direct from sewer pipes into fields at the fringes of the developing world's great megacities." The sewage is added to fields complete with disease-causing pathogens and toxic waste from industry. In some Third World metropolises, all food sold is grown in sewage.[6]

Problems also exist in Europe and the United States. About 20 percent of Europe's rivers and lakes are threatened by con- taminants from industry and agriculture. In Russia, 75 percent

The Purifying Straw

There is a remarkable invention known as the purifying straw to protect people who must rely on water supplies that are not safe. It is a personal, low-cost, portable water purification tool that makes dirty water clean and safe to drink. It is especially effective in the prevention of diarrheal diseases, an all-too-common problem in third world countries. The straw can be used to suck water directly from a water source. As you drink from the straw, a column of iodine resin inside the straw kills bacteria in the water.

The purifying straw is also known as the survival straw. Torben Vestergaard Frandsen came up with the idea ten years ago. Various versions of this device, such as the LifeStraw and the Aquastraw Water Purifier, are sold by different companies. The straw removes most of the microorganisms responsible for causing waterborne diseases.

Until recently, there did not seem to be any practical solution to the problem of providing clean, safe water to the populations of large parts of the Third World. Many poor countries simply lack the resources to develop water purification systems. Electricity to run the equipment is either too expensive or unavailable in many places. The purifying straw now makes it possible to bring clean water to millions of people who might otherwise have died.

A girl uses the LifeStraw, one type of portable purifying straw.

of the inland surface water is polluted, as is 30 percent of the groundwater. In the rural areas of Russia, about 60 percent of the population relies on contaminated wells for their drinking water. In the United States, 40 percent of rivers and streams and 46 percent of lakes are too dangerous for fishing, swimming, or drinking. This sad situation is caused by the huge toxic runoff from large-scale agricultural operations and the widespread use of industrial weed killer.[7]

How Safe Is Our Drinking Water?

Public water systems get water from a variety of locations. These include groundwater (aquifers), surface water (lakes and rivers), rain harvesting, and the sea through desalination. To provide safe drinking water, public water providers must purify the water by disinfecting it. Various chemicals are used. Sometimes water is fluoridated. Surface water may need special treatment.

Today, many people in various parts of the country are concerned about the safety of their drinking water. There have been a number of reports pointing to evidence of contaminants in public water systems. So people wonder just how safe the water from their tap is. The Environmental Protection Agency sets standards for contaminants in public water systems. The United States' water quality is among the world's best. It is regulated by some of the most stringent standards. But some people worry about the chemicals that are used to clean and disinfect our drinking water. In recent years, many have turned to bottled water, believing it to be safer. Unlike tap water, bottled water is regulated by the Food and Drug Administration (FDA). Bottled water is supposed to be the cleanest, purest water, some of it bottled directly from mountain springs. But the fact is that a lot of bottled water is actually tap water. So when you drink bottled water, you can never be sure that what you are drinking is safer than what comes from the tap.

Tap water suppliers publish all their water quality test results. (You can read your local water utility's annual tap water quality report and get information on your city's water in the Environmental Working Group's National Tap Water Atlas.) But bottled water companies do not provide information on such tests.

Bottled water has grown to be a hugely profitable industry. In just one year, 2006, a staggering total of 67.2 billion bottles of water were sold in the United States, 32.6 billion single-serving bottles and 34.6 billion larger bottles.[8] But bottled water is harmful to the environment. Each year, the manufacture of plastic water bottles in the United States requires the use of 17 million barrels of oil.[9] And the transportation of the bottled water wastes a lot of oil, while adding to global warming.

A better choice for those seeking safe water is to buy one of the various water purification systems available for home use. These systems filter out most of the impurities in the water.

The most common systems either use activated carbon filters or reverse osmosis filters. In an activated carbon filtration system, water is purified as it passes through carbon granules or a solid block of carbon. According to Steve Coffel, "No other filtration method is as effective as activated carbon in removing many of the extremely toxic organic chemicals often found in water."[10]

In a reverse osmosis filtration system, water is forced through a plastic membrane. Most contaminants in the water cannot pass through the membrane and are left behind. While both systems have advantages and disadvantages, the best system would be a combination filtration system. This would include reverse osmosis and activated carbon.

From the Reservoir to Your Tap

Many public water supply systems use the following procedure in their treatment plants to purify water before people can drink it. In the typical three-stage system, primary treatment consists of collecting and screening water. Secondary treatment involves removing solids and contaminants using filters and coagulation. And a third treatment stage consists of carbon filtering and disinfection. The treated water is then stored in towers or reservoirs before being fed through the supply system.

Before the water reaches your tap, it must go through pipes. As the water flows through pipes, various dangerous contaminants can enter the water. Many water supply systems are old and have deteriorated over the years. In many places these old pipes may be cracked, and the pipes and pipe joints are full of holes. Toxic substances such as lead and asbestos fibers may leak into such pipes when the water is turned off. Often the anticorrosion treatments contain toxic substances.

Aging asbestos-cement water pipes can pollute the freshwater being distributed in a water system, no matter how pure the

Bottled water has become a huge industry in the United States, but the plastic bottles present an environmental hazard, and the water they contain is often plain tap water.

water may have been to begin with. Asbestos is known to be a dangerous contaminant. Research has indicated that asbestos, if ingested, may increase the risk of cancer of the abdominal tract. There are estimated to be more than 200,000 miles (321,000 kilometers) of asbestos-cement pipe in water distribution systems in the United States. And these water systems are used by an estimated 65 million Americans.[11]

The different types of pipes used to transport water each present unique problems. Lead pipes, used in many older water systems, can add significant amounts of highly toxic lead to the water. This has happened in Washington, D.C., among other places. Forty million Americans currently drink water containing more than the twenty parts per billion maximum contaminant level for lead recommended by the EPA.

Many people believe copper pipes are safe. But the lead solder used with the copper pipes can contaminate drinking water with lead. Water experts recommend that if you have copper pipes in your home, you should let the water run for a minute or so. This will flush out possible contaminants if the water has not been run for awhile.

Plastic pipes are popular in many places. They are used in homes, and water utilities like to use them to replace old pipes. The benefits of plastic pipes include low cost, ease of installation and repair, and best of all—resistance to corrosion. But unfortunately, plastic pipes can pollute your water with the carcinogen vinyl chloride, which is used in its manufacture. Also, many contaminants in the ground can pass directly through the walls of plastic pipes into your water.

How Wastewater Is Treated

Once water is used, wastewater is typically discharged in a sewer system. Pipelines and pumps then transport the water to a wastewater treatment plant. In a properly run modern wastewater treatment plant, systems are designed to mimic natural treatment processes where bacteria consume the organic contaminants in the water. However, in many places, wastewater treatment plants are old and need to be upgraded. For example, wastewater treatment plants are one of the major contributors of nitrogen pollution in the Chesapeake Bay.[12] Officials in the states of the Chesapeake Bay Watershed are aware of the problem, and upgrading the wastewater treatment plants is a primary focus.

The cleaning process in a wastewater treatment plant usually involves two complex treatment stages. In the primary treatment stage, wastewater in flotation tanks is saturated with air. Solid particles that float to the surface are skimmed off. Impurities are also removed from the water. Chemicals known as flocculants are added to the water. The flocculants clump particles together into a mass in a process known as sedimentation. The sediment, called sludge, is removed from the water. It is then hauled away and disposed of either on land or at sea. Sometimes, the sludge is put into airtight tanks. Inside the tanks are anaerobic bacteria (bacteria that exist in the absence of oxygen). The anaerobic bacteria digest the sludge, producing methane gas in the process. The methane can then be used as a fuel, and the leftover sludge may be used as fertilizer.

In the secondary treatment stage, wastewater separated from sludge is aerated. The wastewater is then sprayed onto gravel beds where aerobic bacteria destroy any harmful organic pollutants. In some treatment plants, a third treatment stage is used in which the sedimentation and coagulation processes are repeated. The wastewater is then filtered and disinfected.

After the wastewater is treated, it is discharged into a river, lake, or the sea. But increasingly in many parts of the world, the wastewater is recycled to be reused for landscaping, irrigation, or industrial use.

Recycled Wastewater

A growing number of cities are now recycling wastewater into drinking water. The wastewater is cleaned through additional filtering and chemical treatment after conventional processing is completed. At first, the reaction of residents is usually one of disgust. The image of their water traveling from toilet to tap seems like a terrible idea. Why do we have to drink our own sewage? they ask. Once it is explained to them how the clean water is separated from the polluted water, they accept the situation—as long as the water tastes good.

In many places, especially in dry desert climates, water utilities can no longer keep up with the increasing demand for freshwater from growing populations. Recycling is seen as a logical solution by many water system managers and environmentalists. They agree that the days are over when we can consider wastewater a liability. It is actually an asset. Water has become too valuable to waste. And they intend to figure out how best to use it.

A wastewater treatment plant. In some communities, wastewater is being recycled into drinking water, a practice that concerns some scientists.

However, some scientists have reservations about recycling wastewater for drinking water. Among them is Philip Singer, the Daniel Okun Distinguished Professor of Environmental Engineering at the University of North Carolina.[13] Singer is also director of UNC's Drinking Water Research Center. He believes that recycled water should be used only as nondrinking water. He admits the treatment processes are very good. But he is afraid that trace amounts of dangerous contaminants will escape the multiple physical and chemical filters at the treatment plant. Nevertheless, more and more cities will turn to recycled wastewater to supplement supplies from other traditional sources of freshwater.

Among places already recycling wastewater for drinking water are El Paso, Denver, and Orange County in Southern California. Recycled wastewater is now being discussed as a viable choice in Los Angeles; San Diego; DeKalb County, Georgia; and Miami-Dade County, Florida. The Orange County Water District produces more recycled water than any other water system. It currently produces 70 million gallons (265 million liters) a day, and plans to increase this amount to 85 million gallons (322 million liters) by 2011. No other water system inserts as many physical and chemical barriers between toilet and tap. Writer Elizabeth Royte sampled the Orange County recycled water and reported it to be clean and to taste good.[14]

5

Protecting Our Water

On June 22, 1969, one of the worst things that can ever happen to a river, short of drying up, happened to the Cuyahoga River in Cleveland, Ohio. On that day, the oily Cuyahoga River—probably one of the most polluted rivers in America—burst into flames and burned for about twenty-five minutes. Flames climbed as high as five stories until fireboats brought the fire under control. The fire was believed to have been caused by wastes dumped into the water by industries along the river. Actually, this was not the first time the Cuyahoga River had burned. The river had a long history of fires, at least a dozen of which had occurred since 1868. A fire on the river in 1912 left five men dead.

A fireboat battles the flames on the burning Cuyahoga River in 1952.

In 1952, a fire had caused $1.5 million in damages to boats and a riverfront office building.

The Cuyahoga was not the only river in America to have caught fire. In the first half of the twentieth century, fires burned on the North, Chicago, Buffalo, Fallsaway, Passaic, and Rogue rivers, as well as the Houston Ship Channel. This was a time of rapid industrialization in the United States. Water pollution was seen as an acceptable price to pay for the benefits of industrialization. Concern for shipping and travel on rivers took precedence over pollution. Indeed, the Refuse Act of 1890 actually allowed dumping in the river, as long as it didn't interfere with navigation.

Reports of the 1969 Cuyahoga River fire in the national media suddenly focused attention on the problems and dangers of water pollution in the nation's rivers. Cleveland's Mayor Carl Stokes criticized the federal government for the deplorable condition of the Cuyahoga. He promised to fight for a cleaner river.

The August 1, 1969, edition of *Time* magazine ran an article about the Cuyahoga called "The Price of Optimism." It described the Cuyahoga as "Some river!... Chocolate-brown, oily, bubbling with subsurface gases, it oozes rather than flows."[1] The Federal Water Pollution Control Administration reported that the lower Cuyahoga had "no visible life, not even low forms such as leeches and sludge worms that usually thrive on wastes."[2] Singer-songwriter Randy Newman even wrote a song in 1972 about the Cuyahoga, called "Burn On, Big River."

The 1969 Cuyahoga fire also inspired R.E.M.'s 1986 song "Cuyahoga," and Adam Again's 1992 song "River on Fire."

All the publicity regarding the 1969 Cuyahoga River fire helped spur action to protect the nation's waterways. This activity led to passage of the Federal Water Pollution Control Amendments of 1972, and subsequent legislation aimed at controlling water pollution. Efforts were made to clean up the Cuyahoga and other rivers. In recognition of the improvement in the Cuyahoga's water quality, the Cuyahoga River was designated as one of fourteen American Heritage Rivers in 1998. However, although the river is much cleaner than before, pollution is still a problem. Therefore, the Environmental Protection Agency classified portions of the Cuyahoga River Watershed as one of forty-three Great Lakes Areas of Concern.

Early Efforts to Protect the Nation's Waterways

In the United States, concern over water pollution resulted in the enactment of state antipollution laws in the latter half of the nineteenth century. The first federal government legislation occurred in 1899. The Rivers and Harbors Act is the oldest federal environmental law in the United States.

The Refuse Act of the federal Rivers and Harbors Act of 1899 required obtaining a permit before being allowed to dump wastes into any of the nation's navigable waterways. Today, many activities covered by the Rivers and Harbors Act are regulated by the Clean Water Act. But the Rivers and Harbors Act is still on the books as an independent law, administered by the U.S. Army Corps of Engineers.

The Water Pollution Control Act of 1948 put the Surgeon General in charge of reducing the nation's water pollution.

The Clean Water Act

The Cuyahoga River fire in 1969 resulted in growing public awareness and concern about water pollution. There was a demand to make all the nation's rivers and lakes clean enough for fishing and swimming. To accomplish this, pollution would need to be strictly controlled. The Federal Water Pollution Control Act Amendments of 1972, while strengthening and expanding earlier legislation, brought a change in focus. Previous enforcement was mainly concerned with water quality standards, regulating the amount of pollutants in a given body of water. Priority was now given to establishing procedures for regulating and limiting the amount of pollutants being discharged from particular point sources.

As amended in 1977, the 1972 law became commonly known as the Clean Water Act (often abbreviated as CWA). The Clean Water Act authorized the U.S. Environmental

Protection Agency to establish and enforce wastewater standards for industry. The EPA had recently been established in 1970 to carry out federal laws that were designed to protect the environment.

The CWA introduced a permit system for regulating point sources of pollution. Industries, government facilities such as military bases, and municipal governments would now be required to obtain a permit in order to discharge pollutants into surface waters. The Clean Water Act required technology-based standards for measuring pollution discharge.

The Water Quality Act of 1987

The Clean Water Act had originally failed to include certain nonpoint sources of pollution, exempting these from the permit program. Such sources included urban and industrial stormwater discharges as well as agricultural discharges. Research during the 1970s and 1980s indicated that stormwater discharges were indeed a serious threat to water quality.

Congress enacted the Water Quality Act of 1987 to renew and expand the Clean Water Act. The 1987 act provided funding for communities to build sewage treatment plants and to help clean up the nation's surface water.

Meanwhile, in 1980, the Superfund became law. The program was established to clean up the nation's chemical waste dumps. Funding was increased in 1986, when

A pesticide plant in Fort Valley, Georgia, was named a Superfund site, part of the program enacted by Congress to clean up hazardous waste dumps.

WARNING
NO TRESPASSING

CONTAMINATED AREA
AVOID CONTACT WITH
SOIL AND WATER

FOR INFORMATION
(404) 347-3931

the Superfund was renewed by Congress. The renewal was partly a response to bad news about dangerous chemicals escaping from toxic waste dumps to poison water. When a Superfund site polluted drinking water, the EPA was now required to supply clean water for all household uses, rather than just furnishing purified drinking and cooking water.

In 2002, the CWA was expanded to include the enactment of the Great Lakes Legacy Act. Today, it is still the primary federal law in the United States governing water pollution. While the CWA has made a dramatic difference in U.S. water quality, many problems remain.

Many federal agencies engage in freshwater-related research, administration, projects, oversight, disaster relief, and reconstruction. Water systems managers agree that overall watershed management must be approached in a coordinated manner. But the logistics of such an approach are very difficult because of the huge number of separate agencies, each with their own agendas and sources of funding.

Each of the following agencies are involved in some way with water: the Army Corps of Engineers, the U.S. Fish and Wildlife Service, the Environmental Protection Agency, the National Oceanic and Atmospheric Administration, the Federal Emergency Management Agency, the Council on Environmental Quality, the Food & Drug Administration, the Department of Transportation, the National Park Service, the Agricultural Research Service, the Bureau of Indian Affairs, the Natural

Resources Conservation Service, the Bureau of the Census, the Office of Housing and Urban Development, the Bureau of Land Management, the National Science Foundation, the Small Business Administration, the Bureau of Reclamation, the National Institute of Environmental Health Services, the Economic Development Administration, the State Department's International Boundary and Water Commission, the Rural Utilities Service, and several Department of Homeland Security offices.[3]

The Safe Drinking Water Act

The Safe Drinking Water Act was passed by Congress in 1974, and renewed and strengthened in 1986. The Safe Drinking Water Act requires the Environmental Protection Agency to set standards for drinking-water quality. This means the EPA has to identify drinking water contaminants that could pose a health risk to the American public. The EPA has to define the maximum allowable levels for those contaminants and the treatment techniques to deal with them. The EPA also must establish and carry out enforcement procedures to ensure compliance.

The 1986 version of the Safe Drinking Water Act contained the following new provisions:

* Required each state to develop a program to safeguard the recharge areas of aquifers used by community water systems.

* Called for more comprehensive management of watersheds that supply drinking water.

* Required certain factories, rural schools, and restaurants that have a self-contained water system that furnishes water to at least twenty-five people to meet the act's requirements.

* Banned the use of lead pipes and lead solder in water-supply systems and plumbing systems.

* Made it a federal crime to intentionally introduce a contaminant into or to otherwise tamper with a public water system with the intent of harming its users.

* Tightened the regulation of wastes pumped into the ground through injection wells. Injection wells use high-pressure pumps to place fluid wastes, such as wastewater, brine, or water mixed with chemicals, into porous rock formations deep underground. Groundwater could become contaminated if an injection well developed a leak.

* Established new standards for the treatment of drinking water, such as the requirement of disinfection for all community water systems.

* Established granular activated carbon filtration as the standard to which other water treatment methods will be compared for the filtration of synthetic organic chemicals.

✴ Allowed the use of "point-of-entry" water purification devices, those that purify *all* the water entering the home, as a way for water utilities to meet water purity standards. "Point-of-use devices," those that purify only the water coming out of a single tap, cannot be used to meet the standards.

✴ Required monitoring for some contaminants that are not now regulated.[4]

There are currently more than 160,000 public water systems in the United States. The EPA is required to regulate all of these systems. Each community, in turn, is required to meet the contaminant standards established by the EPA. The agency has classified contaminants into Primary Standards and Secondary Standards. The Primary Standards involve pollutants dangerous to public health and must be complied with.

The Secondary Standards, however, are not enforceable. They are a set of guidelines regarding qualities of water such as taste, odor, and color.

Millions of Americans drink water from systems that are more contaminated than EPA health standards allow.

The states have the option of taking primary responsibility for all the water systems within their borders. All fifty states have chosen to do so rather than have the EPA tell them what steps they must take to meet the federal standards.

Unfortunately, there have been many failures of the Safe Drinking Water Act. The record of enforcement has been poor. Millions of Americans drink water from systems that are more contaminated than EPA health standards allow. And many dangerous pollutants are either not listed or will not be listed for several years. These include organic chemicals, certain radioactive materials, and pathogens, including *Cryptosporidium,* a one-celled parasite that can cause gastrointestinal illness.

In 1993, there was an outbreak of *Cryptosporidium* in Milwaukee. It was estimated to have cost more than $100 million in lost wages, medical costs, and other amounts spent to deal with the crisis. Illnesses caused by drinking contaminated water can be reduced if the regulations under the Safe Drinking Water Act and the Clean Water Act are met.

The Sierra Club recommends the following steps to improve our drinking water:

* Protect watersheds and groundwater from chemical and animal wastes and from erosion due to development.

* Ensure that all large water systems have the basic technologies—sedimentation, coagulation, and/or filtration—to treat drinking water.

* Provide modern technology for water systems that need it.

* Upgrade, improve, or replace crumbling water mains, lead and lead-coated service lines, and leaking waste and sewage lines.

The Pine Street Barge Canal in Burlington, Vermont, is not as peaceful and natural as it appears. The canal was a Superfund site because of pollution from twenty-three different companies along its shore.

The Sierra Club also suggests the following improvements to the Clean Water Act and the Safe Drinking Water Act:

* Enforcing strict environmental protection for watersheds within surface water-supplied drinking water systems and for areas that drain into aquifers used for drinking water.

* Providing financial assistance to needy local public water districts.

✴ Charging about ten cents per 1,000 gallons of water, to be used to fund drinking water cleanup in states that refuse to take action on their own or do not fully fund their own programs.

✴ Providing technical assistance to small systems.

✴ Strengthening requirements of public access to information about drinking water contamination.

✴ Banning all lead in plumbing, faucets, fixtures, and other components that come in contact with drinking water. (Current law allows fixtures to be sold as "lead free" if they contain less than 10 percent lead, which is still enough to contaminate water.)

✴ Increasing the budget for enforcement, state grants, research, and other Safe Drinking Water Act provisions that will help provide all Americans with healthy, safe water from the faucets in our homes.

✴ Strengthening enforcement by the Environmental Protection Agency and state authorities, including higher penalties for noncompliance.[5]

Water Restoration and Conservation

The idea of restoring waterways, rivers, and lakes to a more natural state is relatively new. All over the United States, serious river restoration is under way. Among other measures, this involves the removal of dams that have outlived their usefulness. Communities have been identifying marginal and abandoned dams. They have also questioned the relicensing of dams whose environmental impacts are too costly.

According to writer Elizabeth Grossman:

> It's estimated that less than 1 percent of the nation's river miles are protected in their natural state, and approximately 600,000 miles (965,600 kilometers) of what were free-flowing rivers now lie stagnant behind dams. Virtually no major river in the United States is without a dam. But the nation's dam building peaked in the 1970s, and since 1998, according to the World Commission on Dams, the rate of decommissioning dams in the United States has overtaken the rate of construction.[6]

Dams have, of course, brought many benefits. Because they provide drinking water and hydroelectric power and facilitate flood control, dams have stimulated the growth of urban and agricultural centers in many parts of the country. But dams have proven to be a mixed blessing. More than five hundred in the United States have either been destroyed in the past few years or are scheduled to be shut down. Their environmental costs have been too high. It became clear that these dams were responsible for increased risks of floods, poisoned rivers, harm to aquatic ecosystems, and destruction of fertile farmlands.[7]

In recent years, restoration efforts have also focused on the nation's wetlands. Wetlands are places where the water table is close to the surface, such as swamps and marshes. Some wetland areas are covered with water for part of the growing season and some year-round. Wetlands support plant life that can adapt to saturated soil or watery conditions. Wetlands exist along the coasts in areas of salt water or inland in freshwater.

For centuries, wetlands were believed to be wastelands having very little value. Believing they were useless, Americans destroyed or damaged more than half the nation's estimated 215 million acres of wetlands that originally existed. Wetlands were drained for farming and filled in to build cities. Many of the wetlands were stripped of trees and mined for phosphate and other resources. They were often polluted with toxic wastes or sewage.

But wetlands are very valuable. If allowed to flourish, wetlands can be especially useful in filtering pollution, providing clean water, and reducing flooding. Wetlands have such a remarkable ability to absorb water that, according to the Environmental Protection Agency, a single acre can store between 1 and 1.5 million gallons of floodwater. According to scientists, all a watershed would need to reduce peak floods by 50 percent would be to have 4 to 5 percent of its area in wetland. The Mississippi watershed suffers periodically from disastrous floods. The most extreme floods could be prevented if just 7 percent of the watershed was returned to wetlands. In fact, the greater the area of wetland restoration, the greater the benefits in flood prevention.

Saving the Everglades

At the southern tip of Florida is a huge area of swamps and marshlands known as the Everglades. There are wide expanses of saw grass, a grass with teethlike edges that can grow up to ten feet (three meters) high. Indeed, the Everglades is often called "The River of Grass." There are also tracts of forested land, known as hardwood hammocks. And there are mangroves, trees that grow in salt water along the shoreline.

Development near the Everglades threatens the region's natural beauty and wildlife. The Everglades once covered most of the southern third of Florida. But dikes and canals built early in the twentieth century reclaimed land for farming and housing. The natural flow of water from Lake Okeechobee through the Everglades was restricted. This was a virtual death sentence for the Everglades.

Cut off from much of their water supply, at least half the Everglades' wetlands either were filled in and developed or were left to be overrun with weeds. The Florida panther, manatee, seaside sparrow, and wood stork are just a few of the 68 percent of the Everglades' species on the brink of disappearing. Florida is now eager to undo the damage to the Everglades. It has linked up with the federal government to rebuild the Everglades. Plans call for $7.8 billion in funding for the largest environmental restoration project ever. It may take decades to complete the more than sixty separate construction projects that are planned.[8]

On August 26, 2009, a ruling by a Florida judge allowed the South Florida Water Management District to buy 73,000 acres of farmland from U.S. Sugar Corporation. The district wants to get water flowing again from Lake Okeechobee to the Everglades. It plans to construct a system of water treatment areas and reservoirs on the U.S. Sugar farmland to facilitate the flow of water.[9]

The main reason for the huge restoration project is that Florida is rapidly running out of freshwater. Jeffrey Rothfeder writes:

> With its aquifers dangerously depleted, Florida can't afford to lose forever such a massive, water-rich ecosystem. The state is in a race against time to turn the clock back, to a period when the marshes, swamps, and wetlands of the Everglades on their own, without human intervention, rhythmically and unfailingly distributed water through the area with the precision and consistency of a heartbeat.[10]

A scarlet ibis in the Florida Everglades

Repairing damage from floods can be extremely costly. It is estimated that wetlands, which are so useful in preventing floods, save more than $30 billion a year in repairing flood damage in the United States. Since wetlands are so valuable, protecting them would be a much wiser policy than allowing them to be destroyed and then having to restore them.

The Endangered Species Act, passed by Congress in 1973, requires the government to list and protect all species in the United States in danger of extinction. The government must also protect the habitat of those species. Since wetlands are the habitat of 43 percent of wildlife listed as threatened or endangered, this is yet another reason for protecting valuable wetlands.

In Florida, federal and state policies encouraged the destruction of the state's wetlands for a long time. Florida purchased millions of acres of wetlands and dredged canals or drained them for real estate development and rail lines. Among the unfortunate results of these activities was a lowered water table. This caused the land to sink and soil and vegetation to dry out in many places. And drying conditions caused fire hazards.

Aware of the serious problems in the wetlands, Florida passed a Wetlands Protection Act in 1984. This and other rules were designed to control dredging, conserve fish and wildlife, protect endangered species, and improve water quality. Most states have passed similar laws to regulate wetlands and establish penalties for people who illegally alter wetland habitats.

One important approach to conserving water involves the repairing of pipes that leak badly. A lot of water is also wasted through leaks in irrigation canals and ditches. The irrigation canals and ditches should be repaired. Large irrigation canals can be made of concrete. These steps will go a long way toward reducing the amount of water lost through leaks.

The use of drip irrigation is an excellent way to reduce the amount of water used in agriculture. Israeli agricultural experts developed a computerized system of drip irrigation. Plastic pipes or small tubes, either buried or above ground, have holes that are monitored by computers so that a precise water requirement is delivered to each plant. Unfortunately, this computerized system of irrigation, while effective, is too expensive to use in many places.

Increased conservation may be the best way to solve the water scarcity crisis. Some environmentalists now believe that charging more for water in wealthier countries would encourage conservation. And the money from higher water rates could be used to subsidize the creation of water systems in nations that cannot afford to develop their own.

According to former U.S. senator Paul Simon, "the uncontested reality from cities and farms, in this country and abroad, is that when prices go up, water consumption goes down. The fastest way to bring about water conservation is to make prices realistic."[11]

6

What You Can Do to Help

According to the late senator Daniel Patrick Moynihan of New York, "You can live without oil, and you can live without love. But you can't live without water."[1]

A Green Water Hero

In 1966, the folksinger Pete Seeger, his wife Toshi, and a handful of other river-lovers decided the time had come to try and save New York's Hudson River. For many years, Seeger had gazed down at his beloved river from his mountaintop home in Beacon, New York. Although the river looked beautiful, Seeger knew that it was becoming dangerously polluted. Wouldn't it be wonderful, he thought, if someday the Hudson could again be safe to swim in and its waters clean enough to drink?

Seeger had been a lifelong activist for civil rights and had fought long and hard against war and oppression. Now he directed his energies to saving the environment. Seeger said, "Once upon a time activists concentrated on trying to help the meek inherit the Earth. But we realized that if the Earth wasn't

Folksinger Pete Seeger in front of his sloop, the *Clearwater*. Seeger and his wife, Toshi, began an organization to clean up and preserve the Hudson River.

safe, it wouldn't be more than a garbage dump for the meek to inherit."[2] When asked why he was now focusing on a single river rather than on more weighty issues, Seeger said, "If you save one drop of water, you've saved the world."[3]

Seeger and his friends built a sailboat designed after a one-hundred-year-old sloop. They planned to use the boat to inspire the cleanup of the Hudson River. So they named it the *Clearwater.* Seeger sailed up and down the Hudson, performing music at various towns along the river. He worked hard to educate people about the contamination of the river and how they might fight to clean it up. Clearwater became a nonprofit organization dedicated to preserving and protecting the Hudson River and its ecosystem. Clearwater initiated a twenty-five-year battle with General Electric to remove toxic PCBs from the river. (PCBs, or polychlorinated biphenyls, are a group of synthetic, toxic industrial chemical compounds that were once used in various manufacturing industries. The federal government banned the production of PCBs in 1976 after research revealed the risks they posed to human health, wildlife, and the natural environment.)

Clearwater also played a key role in the passage of the Clean Water Act. The *Clearwater* sloop became an onboard environmental classroom. In the years since *Clearwater* was launched, almost four hundred thousand children have learned all about the Hudson River and its environment while sailing aboard the sloop.

What You Can Do

Who among us has never ever wasted a drop of water? We can all afford to think more, pay attention to our own actions, and change wasteful water habits.

Pete Seeger and others have accomplished amazing things in the struggle to clean up and conserve the nation's waters. But each one of us in our own way can contribute something to this vital ongoing effort. Keep in mind that when it comes to water, each person's daily routine has some impact on the environment. Like Seeger, we can all "save one drop of water."

The most important thing you can do is to conserve water whenever you can. Do not leave the water running while brushing your teeth. Take a shower instead of a bath. And take shorter showers rather than longer ones. Could you collect and use water that would otherwise run down the drain? Could you turn the water on and off in the shower to save water? Encourage your friends and family members to do the same. Ask your parents to install low-flow toilets and showerheads, if your home does not already have them.

How can you tell how much water you use at home? Check the number on your water meter before you leave for school (if no one is home to use water while you are gone), and then check it when you get home. If the two numbers are different, then you have a leak.

Drips, leaks, and letting water run continuously while doing household chores can waste large quantities of water. As much as 20 gallons of water a day can leak from a dripping faucet. And an amazing amount of water can be wasted by a leaking toilet—up to 90,000 gallons a month.

When using a washing machine, always put in a full load of laundry. Also put a full load of dishes in the dishwasher.

Using home water filtration systems is a more environmentally friendly choice than drinking bottled water.

Avoid wasting water when washing dishes by hand by piling the dishes in the sink, filling the sink with water, and then turning off the water.

Do not use bottled water. In most U.S. cities, tap water is usually as good as, if not better than, bottled water. Home water purification systems, however, are safe and can improve the taste of tap water. Meanwhile, plastic bottles are harmful to the environment. Oil is wasted in the manufacture and transport of billions of plastic bottles. Plastic is not biodegradable, and leaching plasticides may be harmful to your health. (Plasticides are chemicals added to plastic to make the plastic softer or more flexible.) If you want to carry your water with you, get a bottle and fill it up.

Keep the water clean. At home, do not pour leftover cleaning agents, paint, solvents, or other chemicals down the drain. Encourage your parents to dispose of these toxic substances at a local household hazardous waste collection facility. Ask your parents to help to organize a neighborhood "Clean Sweep" program to make it easier to dispose of toxic chemicals.

Find out if the water pipes in your school are free of lead. Send for *Lead in School Drinking Water,* available from the Government Printing Office, for a set of recommendations.

If you have a lawn, encourage your parents to use plants that are native to the area and which do not require much water. Because water will evaporate more quickly in warmth and sunlight, water plants at night or during the coolest part of the day. Consider rainwater harvesting as an effective way to conserve water by reusing rainwater for landscaping, gardening, and irrigation. Plants tend to thrive under rainwater irrigation because the water is salt free and relatively free of chemicals. You can collect the rainwater in rain barrels. Rain gardens help stop runoff from impervious surfaces, water that would otherwise be wasted.

> **A dripping faucet can waste 20 gallons of water a day; a leaking toilet can use 90,000 gallons of water in a month.**

Xeriscaping is a landscaping method that uses drought-resistant native plants in an effort to conserve water. If you live in Southern California, Arizona, or any other arid part of the Southwest, surround your house with desert plants rather than grassy lawns.

If you go hiking or camping, protect any freshwater sources from contamination. Also, boil, chemically treat, or filter your drinking water any time you are not sure of water purity. Wash yourself, your clothes, or your dishes at least one hundred feet (thirty meters) away from a natural water source. Use soapless hot water as much as possible. Pour any soapy water into highly absorbent ground.

If you go fishing or boating, stow plastic waste and old fishing gear for proper disposal on land. Where possible, retrieve trash found in the water or on the shore. Organize or participate in local lake, river, or beach cleanup efforts.

What About the Plastic in the Water Bottle?

Whether the source of the water in a plastic water bottle is pure mountain spring water or tap water, the water's quality may be adversely affected by chemicals in the plastic leaching into the water. And some of these chemicals may be harmful to our health. If this is true, why has the use of plastic in the bottled water industry been so widespread? Why have glass bottles been less popular? Well, glass bottles are heavier, so they are not as convenient to carry around. Also, glass bottles can break if dropped, even bottles made of thick glass.

So how can we be safe if we want to use water from plastic bottles? Leaching of chemicals in the plastic can be a problem. This is especially true if the water has been stored in the bottles for a long time. Checking the expiration date on the bottle is always a good idea. Also, be aware that there are different types of plastic bottles, some safe and others not so safe. Some leach and some do not leach.

You can identify what type of plastic bottle you are using by checking the tiny recycling symbol near the bottom of the bottle. Here is what you need to know: #1 stands for polyethylene terephthalate (PET). Most bottled water is sold in this type of bottle. A #1 bottle should only be used once. Use a reusable water bottle instead of refilling a #1 bottle. A #2 high density polyethylene (HDPE), a #4 low density polyethylene (LDPE), and a #5 polypropylene (PP) are all safe to use.

A #7 bottle may leach Bisphenol A (BPA). The colorful, hard plastic Lexan bottles made with polycarbonate plastics are #7 bottles. Bisphenol A has been linked to breast and uterine cancer and type 2 diabetes. It is particularly dangerous for babies and young children. Other bottles to be avoided are those labeled #3 and #6, both of which contain chemicals similar to those in the #7 bottle.[4]

Set up an information table at your school to tell people about the importance of water and conservation and the threats to water quality.

Write a letter to your local or school newspaper in support of specific policies to encourage water conservation and protect water quality.

Check the number on the recycling symbol on your bottle to see if it's safe to use. Those labeled #2, #4, and #5 are fine; avoid bottles labeled #3, #6, or #7.

Send a letter or e-mail to your member of Congress in support of policies that protect water quality. Focus on some aspect of water that particularly interests you.

Ask your parents to make a charitable contribution to one of the nonprofit organizations dedicated to the conservation of water and the protection of water quality.

Ask your local librarian to have a display of water-related books and articles. Ask your teacher to encourage students to make posters about water.

Write a term paper on a topic involving water pollution, conservation, restoration, or scarcity. This is an excellent way to learn more about water.

What Others Are Doing

Many organizations are involved in the effort to reduce water pollution and to help make clean water more available to those who lack access to a reliable supply. One of these organizations, the nonprofit Blue Planet Run Foundation, provides funding and coordinates the efforts of many different groups in various parts of the world. Some of these groups work with the world's poorest people, particularly those living in rural areas. They provide instruction in such simple techniques as how to harvest rainwater and how to make the best use of wells and gravity-fed springs. These pragmatic applications of low-tech solutions are making a difference.

The Blue Planet Run Foundation has a goal of bringing clean and safe water to 200 million people by the year 2027. Toward that end, the foundation's Peer Water Exchange (PWX) is committed to organizing and funding two hundred thousand small peer-managed water projects around the world. Currently PWX has ongoing projects in Bolivia, Honduras, Nicaragua, India, Vietnam, Yemen, Afghanistan, Mali, Ghana, Sierra Leone, and Malawi.

To raise money and educate the public about the global water crisis, the Blue Planet Run Foundation sponsored an around-the-world run in 2007. Twenty-two runners representing thirteen nations participated in this first-of-a-kind athletic event.

Another organization, called charity: water, started by Scott Harrison, has raised $10 million from fifty thousand individual donors in the past three years. The money has been used to provide clean water to nearly one million people in Africa and Asia.[5]

Growing numbers of citizens and groups around the world are fighting for a water-secure future. In our own way, we can each make a difference.

Chapter Notes

Chapter 1. Global Access to Water

1. William Grimes, "Ron Rivera, Potter Devoted to Clean Water, Dies at 60," *New York Times,* September 14, 2008.

2. Marq De Villiers, *Water: The Fate of Our Most Precious Resource* (New York: Houghton Mifflin Company, 2000), p. 11.

3. Maude Barlow and Tony Clarke, *Blue Gold: The Fight to Stop the Corporate Theft of the World's Water* (New York: The New Press, 2002), p. 24.

4. "The Human Body and Water," *U.S. Geological Survey,* October 6, 2009, <http://ga.water.usgs.gov/edu/propertyyou.html> (November 6, 2009).

5. "Water Conservation*," First Unitarian-Universalist Society of Exeter-Green Sanctuary Committee,* 2007, <http://www.exeteruu.org/programs/green.html> (November 6, 2009).

6. "Toward a Sustainable Agriculture," *Center for Integrated Agricultural Systems,* <http://www.clas.wisc.edu/curriculum/modIII/secc/modiii secc act.htm> (November 6, 2009).

7. Barlow and Clarke, p. 8.

8. "Computer Chip Life Cycle," *Environmental Literary Council,* <http://www.enviroliteracy.org/article.php/1275.htm> (November 6, 2009).

9. Jeffrey Rothfeder, *Every Drop for Sale: Our Desperate Battle Over Water in a World About to Run Out* (New York: Penguin Putnam Inc., 2001), p. 173.

10. "How much water is there on, in, and above the Earth?" *USGS Water Science for Schools,* October 20, 2009, <http://ga.water.usgs.gov/edu/earth-howmuch.html> (November 6, 2009).

11. Rothfeder, p. 8.

12. Paul Simon, *Tapped Out: The Coming World Crisis in Water and What We Can Do About It* (New York: Welcome Rain Publishers, 1998), p. 22.

13. Barlow and Clarke, p. 16.

14. Ibid.

15. Ibid., p. 17.

16. Ibid., p. 19.

17. Maude Barlow, *Blue Covenant: The Global Water Crisis and the Coming Battle for the Right to Water* (New York: The New Press, 2007), pp. 4–5.

18. Barlow and Clarke, p. 7.

19. David Carle, *Introduction to Water in California* (Berkeley: University of California Press, 2004), p. 188.

Chapter 2. **Problems of Water Scarcity**

1. Fred Pearce, *When the Rivers Run Dry: Water—The Defining Crisis of the Twenty-First Century* (Boston: Beacon Press, 2006), p. 251.

2. Marq de Villiers, *Water: The Fate of Our Most Precious Resource* (New York: Houghton Mifflin Company, 2000), pp. 12–13.

3. Worldwatch Institute, *Vital Signs 2007–2008: The Trends That Are Shaping Our Future* (New York: W. W. Norton & Company, 2007), p. 50.

4. Pearce, p. 22.

5. "Global Measured Extremes of Temperature and Precipitation," *NOAA Satellite and Information Service,* August 20, 2008, <http://www.ncdc.noaa.gov/oa/climate/globalextremes.html#highpre> (November 6, 2009).

6. "The Effects of Climate Change on Agriculture, Land Resources, Water Resources, and Biodiversity in the United States," Study by the U.S. Department of Agriculture (USDA) and the U.S. Climate Change Science Program, May 27, 2008.

7. Jonathan Amos, science reporter, BBC News, San Francisco, "Arctic summers ice-free 'by 2013'," BBC News, December 12, 2007, <http://news.bbc.co.uk/2/hi/science/nature/7139797.stm> (November 6, 2009).

8. European Commission, Environment DG, July 31, 2009, *Environmental Expert.com,* n.d., <http://www.environmental-expert.com/resultEachPress-Release.aspx?cid=8819&codi=59438&lr=1> (November 6, 2009).

9. Pearce, pp. 123–124.

10. Ibid., p. 124.

11. Ibid., p. 126.

12. Ibid., p. 168.

13. Colorado River Basin: Lifeline of the Southwest, Desert USA, <http://www.desertusa.com/colorado/coloriv/du.coloriv.html>

14. Vandana Shiva, *Water Wars: Privatization, Pollution and Profit* (Cambridge, Mass.: South End Press, 2002), p. 55.

15. Ibid.

16. Pearce, p. 181.

17. Shiva, p. 92.

18. Maude Barlow and Tony Clarke, *Blue Gold: The Fight to Stop the Corporate Theft of the World's Water* (New York: The New Press, 2002), p. 155.

19. Pearce, pp. 248–249.

20. Maude Barlow, *Blue Covenant: The Global Water Crisis and the Coming Battle for the Right to Water* (New York: The New Press, 2007), p. 96.

21. Pearce, p. 250–251.

22. Jeffrey Rothfeder, *Every Drop for Sale: Our Desperate Battle Over Water in a World About to Run Out* (New York: Penguin Putnam Inc., 2001), p. 174.

23. Paul Simon, *Tapped Out: The Coming World Crisis in Water and What We Can Do About It* (New York: Welcome Rain Publishers, 1998), p. 87.

24. Ibid., p. 102.

25. Rothfeder, p. 178.

Chapter 3. **Water Pollution**

1. Loree Griffin Burns, *Tracking Trash: Flotsam, Jetsam, and the Science of Ocean Motion* (Boston: Houghton Mifflin Company, 2007), p. 34.

2. Ibid., p. 39.

3. Associated Press, "Swaths of soupy algae cover Lake Erie," September 21, 2008.

4. "Clean Water and Factory Farms," *Sierra Club,* <http://www.sierraclub.org/factoryfarms> (November 6, 2009).

5. "Gulf of Mexico Dead Zone Smaller Than Expected, But Severe," *ScienceDaily,* July 29, 2009, (November 6, 2009).

6. Geoffrey C. Saign, *Green Essentials: What You Need to Know About the Environment* (San Francisco: Mercury House, 1994), p. 3.

Chapter 4. **Water Quality and Public Health**

1. Marq de Villiers, *Water: The Fate of Our Most Precious Resource* (New York: Houghton Mifflin Company, 2000), p. 101.

2. Steve Coffel, *But Not a Drop to Drink! The Lifesaving Guide to Good Water* (New York: Rawson Associates, 1989), p. 21.

3. Maude Barlow, *Blue Covenant: The Global Water Crisis and the Coming Battle for the Right to Water* (New York: The New Press, 2007), p. 3.

4. Ibid., p. 7.

5. Ibid., p. 10.

6. Ibid., p. 10.

7. Ibid. p. 8.

8. Wendy Williams, "The Bottled Water Con: Buying the Message on the Bottle," November 18, 2008, article for the Land Institute's Prairie Writers Circle, Salina, Kansas.

9. Ibid.

10. Coffel, p. 157.

11. Ibid., p. 48.

12. "Water Pollution in the Chesapeake Bay," *Chesapeake Bay Foundation,* 2009, <http://www.cbf.org/Page.aspx?pid=913> (November 6, 2009).

13. Elizabeth Royte, "A Tall, Cool Drink of … Sewage?" *New York Times Magazine,* August 10, 2008.

14. Ibid.

Chapter 5. **Protecting Our Water**

1. Loretta Neal, "Burned Into History: The Cuyahoga River Fires," *Balanced Living Magazine,* Medina, Ohio, 2008.

2. Quote from August 1, 1969, *Time* magazine mentioned in "The Cuyahoga River Fire of 1969," Pratie Place, March 16, 2005, <http://pratie.blogspot.com/2005/03/cuyahoga-river-fire-of-1969.html> (November 6, 2009).

3. Elizabeth de la Vega, "Our National Water Policy … Oh, Wait, We Don't Have One," July 23, 2008, <http://www.tomdispatch.com/post/174958/elizabeth_de_la_vega_those_hard_rains_are_gonna_fall> (November 6, 2009).

4. Steve Coffel, *But Not a Drop to Drink! The Lifesaving Guide to Good Water* (New York: Rawson Associates, 1989), pp. 187–188.

5. Scott Alan Lewis, *The Sierra Club Guide to Safe Drinking Water* (San Francisco: Sierra Club Books, 1996), pp. 81–83.

6. Elizabeth Grossman, *Watershed: The Undamming of America* (New York: Counterpoint, 2002), p. 3.

7. Jeffrey Rothfeder, *Every Drop for Sale: Our Desperate Battle Over Water in a World About to Run Out* (New York: Penguin Putnam Inc., 2001), p. 142.

8. Ibid., pp. 141–142.

9. Andy Reid, "Judge allows Crist's Everglades land deal to move forward," *South Florida Sun-Sentinel,* August 26, 2009.

10. Rothfeder, p. 142.

11. Paul Simon, *Tapped Out: The Coming World Crisis in Water and What We Can Do About It* (New York: Welcome Rain Publishers, 1998), p. 127.

Chapter 6. What You Can Do to Help

1. Steve Coffel, *But Not a Drop to Drink! The Lifesaving Guide to Good Water* (New York: Rawson Associates, 1989), p. 15.

2. "The Rescue of a River: Pete Seeger Is Still at It," *New York Times,* September 6, 2008.

3. Jeffrey Rothfeder, *Every Drop for Sale: Our Desperate Battle Over Water in a World About to Run Out* (New York: Penguin Putnam Inc., 2001), p. 191.

4. Vreni Gurd, "Which plastic water bottles don't leach chemicals?" *Trusted. MD,* Nutrition & Life, March 29, 2007, <http://trusted.md/blog/vreni_gurd/2007/03/29/plastic_water_bottles> (November 6, 2009).

5. Nicholas D. Kristof, "Clean Sexy Water," *New York Times,* July 12, 2009.

Glossary

acid rain—Rain with increased acidity caused by atmospheric pollution.

acre-foot—The amount of water required to cover an area of one acre to a depth of one foot; equal to 325,851 gallons.

activated carbon filter—A system of water purification.

algae—Primitive plants having one or many cells and usually adapted to water.

aqueduct—A channel or pipe for carrying water.

aquifer—An underground layer of rock, sand, or gravel that contains groundwater that can be drawn out for use above ground.

atmosphere—The area surrounding the earth, including three chief layers: the troposphere, stratosphere, and mesosphere.

biodegradable—Capable of being broken down biologically into basic elements through the action of microorganisms such as bacteria.

blowout—The uncontrolled release of oil from an offshore well.

brine—Water with a very high dissolved-mineral or salt content.

cloud seeding—Causing raindrops to form by seeding clouds with silver iodide crystals.

confined aquifer—An aquifer that is trapped between two impermeable layers of material.

conservation—Protecting something so that it is not used up or spoiled.

contaminant—A substance that pollutes.

current—A large body of water moving in a certain direction.

dead zone—An area of the sea with a condition known as hypoxia, where there is too little oxygen to support all forms of marine life.

delta—The area where a river flows into the sea.

desalination—The process of removing salts from seawater to produce freshwater.

distillation—A method of purifying water by evaporation and condensation.

drip irrigation—A direct, water-saving method of nourishing plants. Drip systems trickle water to plant roots from small holes in pipes.

drought—A long period of dry weather.

ecosystem—A community of living things together with the environment in which they live.

estuary—The mouth of a large river.

evaporate—To change water from a liquid to a gas (vapor).

flocculants—Chemicals added to wastewater that cause particles to clump together during treatment process.

fossil fuels—Fuels such as oil, gas, and coal that are formed in the earth from plant or animal remains.

glacier—A huge mass of ice that moves slowly down mountain valleys or over land.

groundwater—Water that lies below the water table.

hydroelectric power—Electric power that is generated by water flowing over a dam.

hydrological cycle—The water cycle; the various paths and forms that water takes as it circulates through the air to the earth and back again.

irrigation—Diverting water resources with channels, ditches, canals, or dams to agricultural areas that lack enough rainfall for crops.

nonpoint source pollution—Pollution emitted along a wide boundary, such as a landfill, mining site, or farmland.

pathogens—Disease-causing organisms, such as bacteria and viruses.

plastic—Any of a number of petroleum-based products that do not biodegrade.

point source pollution—Pollution from a specific point, such as a pipe.

precipitation—Rain or snow.

rainwater harvesting—Collecting rainwater in cisterns or tanks in the ground.

recycled water—Water that is used again.

reservoir—A place where people store water for later use.

reverse osmosis—A method of purifying water by forcing it through semipermeable filters.

sludge—The solid part of sewage.

toxic—Poisonous.

tributaries—Small rivers or streams that flow into larger ones.

unconfined aquifer—An aquifer that has the water table as its upper boundary.

wastewater—Water that has been used.

watershed—A natural area that funnels water into rivers and lakes.

water table—The level below which the earth is saturated with water.

wetlands—Very wet low-lying areas, such as swamps or marshes.

xeriscaping—Using local native plants and vegetation in gardens and lawns.

For More Information

American Oceans Campaign
1350 Connecticut Ave. NW,
5th Floor
Washington, DC 20036

American Rivers
1101 14th St. NW, Suite 1400
Washington, DC 20005

Center for Marine Conservation
1725 DeSales St. NW
Washington, DC. 20036

Clean Water Action
1010 Vermont Ave. NW,
Suite 1100
Washington, DC 20005-4918

Environmental Defense Fund
1875 Connecticut Ave. NW
Washington, DC 20009

Freshwater Society
2500 Shadywood Rd.
Excelsior, MN 55331

Friends of the Earth
1717 Massachusetts Ave.,
Suite 600
Washington, DC 20036

Greenpeace USA
702 H St. NW
Washington, DC 20001

Kids for Saving Earth
37955 Bridge Rd.
North Branch, MN 55056

National Oceanic and
Atmospheric Administration
1401 Constitution Ave. NW
Room 5128
Washington, DC 20230

National Resources Defense
Council
40 W. 20th St.
New York, NY 10011

The Nature Conservancy
4245 North Fairfax Dr.
Suite 100
Arlington, VA 22203-1606

Oceanic Society
Fort Mason Quarters 35
San Francisco, CA 94123

Sierra Club
408 C Street NW
Washington, DC 20002

U.S. Environmental Protection
Agency
Ariel Rios Building
1200 Pennsylvania Ave. NW
Washington, DC 20460

Worldwatch Institute
1776 Massachusetts Ave. NW
Washington, DC 20036-1904

Further Reading

Arato, Rona. *World of Water: Essential to Life.* New York: Crabtree Publishing, 2005.

Burns, Loree Griffin. *Tracking Trash: Flotsam, Jetsam, and the Science of Ocean Motion.* Boston: Houghton Mifflin Company, 2007.

Fridell, Ron. *Protecting Earth's Water Supply.* Minneapolis: Lerner Publications, 2009.

Spilsbury, Richard. *Managing Water.* Chicago: Heinemann Library, 2008.

Internet Addresses

Environmental Protection Agency
<http://www.epa.gov>

The Hydrologic Cycle
<http://www.iwr.msu.edu/edmodule/water/cycle.htm>

Water Science for Schools
<http://ga.water.usgs.gov/edu/>

Index

A

access, issues in, 6–9, 71–72
acid rain, 63–65
activism
    Clearwater, 104–106
    how you can help, 107–113
    organizations generally, 113–114
Africa, 6–9, 22, 26, 27, 34, 73
agriculture. *See also* irrigation.
    groundwater pumping for, 17
    pollution from, 28, 53–55, 60, 89
    programs to benefit, 20
    runoff, 58–60
    wastewater, 42, 73
    water's importance to, 7, 9, 22, 26, 35
algal blooms, 53
aquifers, 13–17, 30, 55–58
arsenic poisoning, 72
artesian aquifers, 13
asbestos pipes, 78–79

B

blowouts, 61
bottled water, 76, 109, 111

C

CALFED, 19–22
California, 17, 19–22, 36, 46
Canada, 26, 68–69
China, 7, 26, 38, 41–42, 71
cholera, 7, 71, 73

Clean Water Act, 88–89, 95–96, 106
cloud seeding, 43
Colorado River, 16, 26, 36–37
conservation
    CALFED, 19–22
    government agencies, 91–92, 94
    history of, 87–88
    legislation, 88–97, 102
    overview, 19
    restoration, 97–103
copper pipes, 79
Cryptosporidium, 95
Cuyahoga River fire, 84–87, 88

D

dams, 36, 97–98
dead zones, 58–60
desalination, 44–48
deserts, 23–25, 27
dioxin, 69
diseases, 6–7, 58, 70–75
distillation, 46
droughts, 7, 27, 28

E

Egypt, 12, 35
estuary, 21
Everglades, 100–101
Exxon Valdez, 61

F

factory farms, 56
Federal Water Pollution Control Amendments of 1972, 87, 88

fog catchers, 23–25
fossil fuels, 28, 47,
freshwater
    access, issues in, 6–9, 71–73
    cycling of, 12–19
    depletion of, 16–19
    distribution, 10–11
    safety of, 75–77
    scarcity. *See* scarcity of
        freshwater.
    uses of, 9, 11–12

G

gasoline storage tanks, 57–58
glaciers, 11, 31–32
global warming, 27–31, 47, 60,
    76
Great Pacific Garbage Patch,
    49–52
greenhouse gases, 28, 29, 47
groundwater, 12–18, 55–58, 70,
    72, 75 93

I

India, 12, 34, 36, 41, 71
irrigation
    as contributor to scarcity, 12,
        15–16
    drip, 22, 103
    rainwater, 110
    techniques, improving, 22
Israel, 32, 43, 45, 46

J

Jordan, 32, 43

L

leaching, 58, 109, 111

lead pipes, 79, 93
Love Canal, 68–70

M

management, challenges in,
    20–22
methane, 28, 81
Mexico, 17, 36

N

National Water Carrier, 33
Nile River, 12, 35
nitrous oxide, 28
North Polar region, 30

O

oceans (salt water), 10, 44
Ogallala aquifer, 15–17
oil spills, 60–63
overpopulation, 18–19, 25–27

P

perchloroethylene (PCE), 66
pipes, 78–80, 93, 109
pollution
    acid rain, 63–65
    from agriculture, 28, 53–55,
        60, 89
    brine, 47–48
    dead zones, 58–60
    groundwater, 55–58
    health effects, 66–70
    oil spills, 60–63
    plastic, 49–52, 76, 109, 111
    point source, 53, 88–89
    sources of, 52–55
precipitation, 14, 25–27, 31
Primary Standards, 94

privatization of water resources, 38–41

public-private partnerships, 38–41

purification
    ceramic water filters, 4–6
    filtration, 76–77
    point-of-use devices, 93–94
    public water supply, 77–80, 93, 94

purifying (survival) straw, 74

reverse osmosis, 46, 77

R

rain harvesting, 41, 75

rain-making, 42

Refuse Act of 1899, 87

reverse osmosis, 46, 77

Rivers and Harbors Act, 87–88

S

Safe Drinking Water Act, 92–97

scarcity of freshwater
    global warming, 27–31, 76
    overpopulation, 18–19, 25–27
    overview, 6–7, 12, 16, 22
    solutions to, 41–48
    water wars, 32–41

Secondary Standards, 94

sewage systems, 58

Six-Day War, 32

sound, rain-making by, 42

sprinkler systems, 22

standards, 94

subsidence, 17

Sudan, 27, 35

Superfund, 89–91

T

Three Gorges Dam, 38

toxic waste dumping, 66–70, 109

trichloroethylene (TCE), 66

typhoid, 6–7, 71

U

United States, 6, 9–10, 12, 15, 29, 30, 73

W

wastewater
    agriculture, 42, 73
    recycling, 42, 81–83
    treatment, 80–81

water cycle, 14

Water Quality Act of 1987, 89–92

watersheds, 13

water table, 13

West Antarctic Ice Sheet, 30

wetlands, 7, 13, 20, 98–102

wet scrubbers, 65

X

xeriscaping, 110

Y

Yangtze River, 37–38

Yellow River, 12